MW00862003

OUT OF OLD
ONTARIO
KITCHENS

Lindy Mechefske

Copyright 2018 Lindy Mechefske

All rights reserved. No part of this book covered by the copyrights hereon may be reproduced or used in any form or by any means – graphic, electronic, or mechanical – without the prior written permission of the publisher. Any request for photocopying, recording, taping, or information storage and retrieval systems of any part of this book shall be directed in writing to the Canadian Reprography Collective, 379 Adelaide Street, West, Suite M1, Toronto, Ontario, M5V 1S5.

MacIntyre Purcell Publishing Inc.
194 Hospital Rd.
Lunenburg, Nova Scotia
B0J 2C0
(902) 640-3350

www.macintyrepurcell.com
info@macintyrepurcell.com

Printed and bound in Canada by Friesens

Design and layout: Denis Cunningham
Cover design: Denis Cunningham

Cover Image: Apple Blossoms, Victorian Card, The Old Design Shop (olddesignshop.com)

ISBN : 978-1-77276-112-2

Library and Archives Canada Cataloguing in Publication

Mechefske, Lindy, author Out of Old Ontario Kitchens / Lindy Mechefske.

ISBN 978-1-77276-112-2 (hardcover)

1. Cooking, Canadian--Ontario style--History. 2. Cooking-- Ontario--History. 3. Frontier and pioneer life--Ontario.   4. Cookbooks. I. Title.

TX715.6.M435 2018   641.59713   C2018-903462-9

MacIntyre Purcell Publishing Inc. would like to acknowledge the financial support of the Government of Canada and the Nova Scotia Department of Tourism, Culture and Heritage.

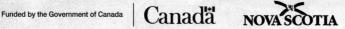

For all the women who went before us,
working relentlessly, paving the way.

For my beloved daughters, Laura and Elly.

And for my paternal grandfather, Harry Sutcliffe,
who taught me while I was yet a toddler,
about the intersection of food and love.

TABLE OF CONTENTS

A NOTE ABOUT THE SCOPE OF THIS BOOK

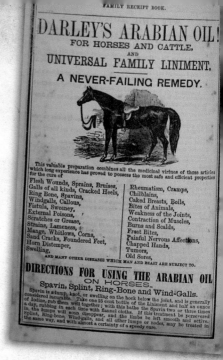

FAMILY RECEIPT BOOK.

DARLEY'S ARABIAN OIL!
FOR HORSES AND CATTLE,
AND
UNIVERSAL FAMILY LINIMENT.
A NEVER-FAILING REMEDY.

This valuable preparation combines all the medicinal virtues of those articles which long experience has proved to possess the most safe and efficient properties for the cure of

Flesh Wounds, Sprains, Bruises, Galls of all kinds, Cracked Heels, Ring Bone, Spavin, Windgalls, Callons, Fistula, Sweeney, External Poisons, Scratches or Grease, Strains, Lameness, Mange, Whitlows, Corns, Sand Cracks, Foundered Feet, Horn Distemper, Swelling,

Rheumatism, Cramps, Chilblains, Caked Breasts, Boils, Bites of Animals, Weakness of the Joints, Contraction of Muscles, Burns and Scalds, Frost Bites, Painful Nervous Affections, Chapped Hands, Tumors, Old Sores,

AND MANY OTHER DISEASES WHICH MAN AND BEAST ARE SUBJECT TO.

DIRECTIONS FOR USING THE ARABIAN OIL
ON HORSES.
Spavin, Splint, Ring-Bone and Wind-Galls.

Spavin is a lump, knot, or swelling on the hock below the joint, and is generally considered incurable. Take one 25 cent bottle of the Liniment and half an ounce of Iodine, rub them well together; with this bathe the Spavin two or three times a day, rubbing in each time with flannel cloths. If this treatment be persevered in, the lumps will soon disappear, and the limbs be left smooth and active. Splint, Ring-bone, Wind-galls, and all other lumps or nodes, may be treated in the same way, and with almost a certainty of a speedy cure.

The timeline of this book focusses primarily on the 1800s and early 1900s but extends earlier where possible, to include the long era of human habitation before European contact and concludes a decade after the end of the Second World War.

In part the 1950s were chosen as an end point because from the 1960s on, our foodways changed dramatically with the increasing mechanization of farming; the expanding availability of supermarkets and commercially prepared foods; and the beginnings of the wide-spread growth of the fast-food sector, including for example the first Tim Hortons donut shop, which opened in Hamilton in 1964.

It would be folly to assume that one book could cover all aspects of the culinary history of this vast and ancient land. Ontario is over a million square kilometres in area – larger than both France and Spain combined. And, like the rest of Canada, it is one of the most multicultural places on Earth. Toronto has been called the most ethnically diverse city in the world: home to immigrants from almost every country and religious group.

Most of the recipes included here come from historic sources that were either published in Ontario or are from books that would have been used by settlers in Upper Canada. As many recipes as possible, though, come from private collections and are identified as such.

The British Influence
Because we are all migrants here, except for the Indigenous Peoples, many of the recipes come from away – the only criteria for selecting them, outside of the stated timeline (pre-contact to a decade after the Second World War) was that they had an Upper Canadian or Ontario connection. It is hard to escape the British influence in early Upper Canadian cuisine – in part because Canada was a British colony predominantly settled by the British in the early years; but also because most of the cookbooks of the era were written in English.

Some of the recipes appear in their original form, with Imperial or other measurments (butter the size of a hen's egg, etc.). A conversion chart has been included to help interpret the old recipes. In some cases, modern interpretations have been included and are noted as such, otherwise the recipes are as they would have appeared, in both old cookbooks and private recipe collections.

Other criteria for selecting recipes was that they needed to be feasible, meaning the ingredients needed to be available. Except in a couple of cases, recipes calling for ingredients such as calves' heads, pigs' heads, plovers, larks, cow heels, pigs feet, turtles, pearlash, potash, beef heart, tripe, and other unlikely ingredients were not included. For anyone interested, those recipes can easily be found in most cookbooks from the 1800s.

"I don't know why old recipes are so evocative, since many of the ingredients are unknown to me or difficult to get, the processes laborious beyond belief, and the results, quite honestly, often nothing I'd want to eat. But they read like a poetry of lost specifics..."

John Griswold, "Turkey, A Love Story,"
Inside Higher Ed.

INTRODUCTION

In high school history class, I remember rote learning the dates of battles; the names of the early, all-male, all-white explorers; and, as the new nation of Canada began to emerge, the names of our first politicians – also all-white, all-male.

The only time I perked up was at the mention of pemmican, bannock, maple syrup, salt pork, or dried-salted fish. Or by how anyone survived winter without electricity, central heat, and indoor plumbing. I was fascinated not by colonial politics, nor the battles fought, nor by the horrendous ransacking of land, which was scarcely referenced, but by how Indigenous Peoples and settlers lived and survived, what they ate, and where their food came from: the most crucial of details that were rarely mentioned.

Backtrack a few years earlier and I was a brand new Canadian, my family having just emigrated from England. Decades later, the thing I remember most clearly was the profound sense of longing for tastes of a life left behind. For the times I'd spent as a very young girl, helping my beloved grand-father in his ancient Yorkshire kitchen – shelling peas, learning to knead bread dough and roll out pastry for jam tarts, and watching the Yorkshire puddings rise in the oven as the Sunday roast rested on the counter.

A Powerful Symbol

Food was one of the most noticeable changes in my life on arrival in Ontario. Suddenly I was immersed in a world of Wonder Bread, corn on the cob, pop tarts, burgers, and hot dogs. I learned very young that how we cook and what we eat – our food – is a powerful symbol of our culture, history, and identity, and one of our most meaningful connections to our past.

Food is central to our history. Cooking too. Cooking is what makes humans unique. It is the truly critical part of our history as a race, the thing that differentiates us from every other species. Cooking connects us to our past, to our bloodlines, and all the way back to our ancient human forebears, likely Homo erectus, whom, it is thought, started cooking 1.8 million years ago, forever changing the course of human destiny.[1]

Food is fundamental – the world's largest industry. Food and cooking are about our very survival as a species. And yet, curiously, we've largely ignored our culinary history. Perhaps that's partly because, for centuries, except in the most exceptional circumstances, it was women who were the keepers of food knowledge.

It was women who got up and lit the fire in the hearth, and toiled and stirred and cooked and baked, who fed babies and kept families alive. Women who put down food for long, hard winters and who fed communities through plagues and depressions, famines and wars. For the longest time, until the mid to late 1900s, it was women who did the vast majority of the cooking.

Everything from Scratch

The truth was, and still is, the preparation of food is no small task. That was especially so for the earliest settlers, who had access to few ingredients; ate only what they could grow, gather, hunt or otherwise find locally and seasonally; preserved as best they could given their limited means and even the vessels to do so; cooked on open hearths; and made everything from scratch.

In the earliest days, even the grain had to be hand ground for flour before bread could be made. The preservation, preparation, and cooking of food was all consuming, crucial, vital, life-sustaining work, every bit as important as farming, mining, commerce, politics, and the development of infrastructure – none of which really mattered without someone to prepare the food.

These are the unsung stories of the women who went before us – our mothers and aunts, our grandmothers and great-grandmothers and great-great grandmothers and so on – of their talent, creativity, thought, care, relentless hard work, and incredible ingenuity in the kitchen. Food runs like a perpetual thread through the lives of generations of women, stretching back to a time we can no longer remember, and forward to a time we cannot even imagine.

It was also women who wrote down the recipes; who wrote, compiled, and annotated cookbooks; who kept diaries with exquisite details of the food they prepared and ate; and who passed on the sacred knowledge – the special code. Little did they know that they were quietly recording some of the most fundamental details of history – that is – how we ate and lived and survived.

Overlooked and Undervalued

The early female food writers produced cookbooks that are both a much overlooked and undervalued literary tradition but also a tremendously important primary history source. Books were then, as they are now, fundamentally important. During the late 1700s and early 1800s, books were few and far between in most settlers' homes. A family on the land might be lucky to have a Bible and perhaps a cookbook.

Many a young woman developed not only her culinary abilities, but also her literacy and numeracy skills, thanks in good measure to the availability of a cookbook. Cookbooks were personal – an intimate, private workspace where all kinds of details could be recorded, and lessons learned – where their owners could connect to the world at large, and to a body of knowledge both practical and creative.

Culinary history is finally finding its rightful place. And it's not just the relatively short period of colonial culinary history that we're learning about, but also the vast stretches of time before European contact, when ancient Indigenous populations around the world hunted and fished, cultivated crops, and developed an elaborate knowledge of the natural world.

Food is Life

Food played a huge and vital role in the history and building of the province of Ontario. A significant portion of our economic prosperity was, and is, tied to our ability to grow, harvest, produce, and distribute food. But, food is not just an industry. We eat because it is a biological necessity; because food is life. But food is also about hunger and yearning; about memory and love; about life and death; about history and power; about community and belonging, and about the powerful connections between us.

It has been such a privilege to travel throughout this province talking culinary history with so many and spending time immersed in the diaries of the early settlers, poring over rare old cookbooks, and holding in my hands delicate and even rarer, old manuscript cookbooks, handwritten in copperplate on fragile, yellowed pages blurred with time and the traces left behind – drips and splatters and cryptic scrawled notes – the tangible, touching, and poignant evidence of the women who went before us.

I am grateful and indebted to the curators and archivists and librarians who helped me along my way. And, to the many people who invited me into their homes and shared their treasured family recipes and stories – thank you for your remarkable generosity.

Food stories, it turns out, are the real stories of our lives.

(Bottom) Cooking Class, Ladies College, Ottawa, August 1906, by William James Topley.

In the Beginning

Long before the massification of food – that is, before industrial farming and mono-cultures; before fast food and before colossal supermarkets began selling standardized foods year-round; before factory foods and food shipped thousands of miles on freeways and in airplanes; before electricity and before the industrial revolution; and before the colonization of the world – we hunted and fished, gathered and farmed, cooked and ate. Food was our primary occupation.

Our foods were simple, seasonal, local, specific to our regions. We were dependent on the naturally occurring plants, the waters we fished from, the forests and plains where we hunted the animals and birds that we lived amongst, and eventually, the soils in which we could grow things. Once upon a time, we ate to live. Now we live to eat.

In the beginning, the land now called Ontario, was one immense woodland forest, intercepted only by thousands of crystal-clear lakes and rivers, the ranging, rocky outcroppings of the Canadian Shield, and the odd natural clearing where the soil was more conducive to growing wild grasses.

Since 10,000 BCE

Here in the wilderness, the First People lived and roamed for thousands of years. We don't know with absolute certainty when or where these early people came from, but we do know that they came so long ago that they should be called Indigenous. The dates are almost impossible to comprehend. Recent evidence suggests that there have been early Palaeolithic peoples in Ontario since 10,000 BCE, and possibly longer.[2]

There are many distinct Indigenous nations, cultures, and languages in Ontario including a small population of Inuit; one hundred and thirty-three First Nations communities including the Anishinaabe, Haudenosaunee, and Cree; and since the arrival of European settlers, the Métis.

The Indigenous people who lived here were, to varying degrees, hunters, fishers, and gatherers – all of them remarkably adept at survival. Some groups were nomadic and others had highly organized structured villages and societies. Some were advanced agricultural societies. All had a sophisticated knowledge of the natural world and an oral tradition of storytelling, spirituality, music, and sharing of sacred knowledge, which were passed on generation to generation through the Elders.

The First Peoples were also makers: sewing elaborate, beautiful, and highly functional clothes using animal skins and sinews; making tools for hunting and clay vessels for cooking; weaving baskets from rushes and grasses; using bones to make tools and fasteners; inventing and building canoes using birch bark, cedar wood, and spruce gum; making medicines from plants; tapping maple trees for sap and cooking it to make syrup and sugar; preserving meat by drying and smoking it; gathering and drying wild fruits and nuts; and for thousands of years, harvesting wild rice, the only native cereal grain found in Canada. They grew corn, squash, beans, tobacco and other crops. By the 1700s, the Algonquians had apple orchards in Southern Ontario.[3]

Glittering Water

The marks of the First Nations, Inuit and Metis are everywhere in this land; in the crops we still grow, in our diets, on the land itself, and in our language and customs. Even the word Ontario is itself Wyandot (Huron) in origin – thought to mean beautiful or glittering waters – an apt name since Ontario's 250,000 plus lakes contain about one fifth of the world's fresh water.

The first Europeans to arrive in Ontario were three white men. The first of these, a mere 16-year-old boy, was French explorer Étienne Brûlé (c. 1592 –1633), who arrived in 1608 and spent much of his life amongst the Hurons or Wendat people, from whom he learned the language and culture.

Next came English explorer, Henry Hudson, (c. 1565–1611) in 1609. Hudson, for whom the Hudson River, Hudson Bay, and the Hudson's Bay Company (founded in 1670) are all named, met an unfortunate early end after a miserable winter on the shore of James Bay, when the crew mutinied and cast Hudson and his son, John, and seven other crew members adrift, never to be seen again.

French navigator, cartographer, and explorer. Samuel de Champlain (c. 1574 – 1635), who founded New France and Quebec City in 1608, was the third European to arrive in what was to become Upper Canada, landing in 1615. His travels took him throughout the province and eventually to the region around Lake Huron, where he paved the way for French missionary outposts, including Sainte-Marie among the Hurons, established in 1639.

Henry Hudson 1565–1611

The French established a presence in many areas of the province, but in 1763, Britain won the Seven Years' War and took full control of Upper Canada, which was officially established in 1791 by the Kingdom of Great Britain.

The First Immigrants

The first major wave of immigration to Canada occurred in 1784, when tens of thousands of Loyalists who supported the British cause during the American Revolution (1775-1783) fled the United States and headed north into Canada. Among the Loyalists were clergy, clerks, lawyers, soldiers, college graduates, farmers, tradespeople, families with young children, new European immigrants to the United States, Blacks, escaped slaves, and about 2,000 Indigenous allies who were mainly Six Nations Iroquois.

Between 7,500 and 9,000 Loyalists, enticed by land grants from the Crown, ended up resettling in Upper Canada, living in communities along the St. Lawrence River including Kingston and along Lake Ontario from the Bay of Quinte to Hamilton and throughout the Niagara Peninsula. Other Loyalist settlements included those along the Detroit and Thames Rivers and also at Long Point. The Iroquois Loyalists settled along the Grand River. The arrival of the Loyalists added many English speakers to the Upper Canadian population, marking a distinct change in the history of the province.

The Loyalists' arrival and the settlements they created changed the face of the land forever. So profound was the Loyalist impact that the motto on the Coat of Arms for Ontario, *Ut incepit Fidelis sic permanet*, Latin for, "Loyal she began, loyal she remains," refers to the Loyalist refugees who settled in Upper Canada.

Mill on the Gananocoui [ca. 1792], by Elizabeth Simcoe.

The Pennsylvania Dutch Farmers

The Loyalists were soon followed by the migration of thousands of industrious Pennsylvania Dutch farmers (Deutsch from Germany, not the Netherlands), who migrated from Pennsylvania to Upper Canada bringing their farming knowledge and a great reverence for food. Many of the Pennsylvania Dutch immigrants were Lutheran and German Reformed but there were also large groups of Anabaptists including Mennonites, Amish and Hutterites.

The first group of Mennonites migrated to Upper Canada in 1786, settling primarily in the Waterloo region. They were followed by a number of Quakers. In 1793, the British government promised them exemption from military service.

Following the war of 1812, when Upper Canadian forces (including British and Canadian forces and First Nations warriors) defeated invading American troops, a period of stability saw the rise of European – predominantly English, Scottish, and Irish – migration to Upper Canada. Around the same time, enslaved African-Americans began arriving in Canada and by the 1830s the term Underground Railroad was coined, coinciding with the growth of various railway systems being built. In all, an estimated thirty to forty thousand individuals found their way to freedom via a series of routes through Upper and Lower Canada.

Map of Canada West 1855, from Colton, J. H., and Colton, G. W., *Colton's Atlas of the World Illustrating Physical and Political Geography, Vol 1*, New York, 1855 (First Edition).

By 1841, Upper Canada had been renamed Canada West, a name that never really took hold. It was the creation of the Dominion of Canada on July 1st, 1867, under the British North America Act, that saw the province renamed Ontario, one of the first four provinces of Canada, along with Quebec, Nova Scotia and New Brunswick.

From that time forward, for decade after decade, enticed by land, by opportunity, and by freedom, wave after wave of immigrants followed from all over the world. From the 1850s on, right through to the Great Depression, there were the Kashubs who settled in the Madawaska and Bonnechere Valleys, and influxes of Scandinavian, Russian, German, Polish, Ukrainian, Serbian, and Italian immigrants, dispersing throughout the province – some groups settling in the north attracted by jobs in mining and lumber operations and others heading straight to the urban centres in the south. At the end of the Second World War, growing numbers of Asian and Latin American immigrants began arriving.

The Evolving Kitchen

The 1800s marked an incredible pace of change in the world and perhaps nowhere was this more apparent than in the kitchen. At the beginning of the 1800s, Upper Canadian kitchens were primitive affairs with open hearths, candle and lantern lighting, and few easy means of safely storing food. Cooking was a laborious, time-consuming, and relentless job. Everything had to be made from scratch including the starter with which to make bread.

Breadmaking alone was a near-perpetual occupation for most settlers – almost always the women. Many settlers lived on the land and had limited access to towns or grocery stores. Ontario's long, cold winters meant that food preparation and preservation were paramount for survival.

By the end of the 1800s, new canals and railways throughout Ontario meant that the province was quickly opening up and access to provisions and ingredients was expanding rapidly. Thomas Edison had invented the electric light bulb; most Ontario kitchens had cast iron cooking stoves; and though not yet readily available, the world's first electric oven had been invented, right here in Ontario.

In addition, tin cans had become prevalent, Mason jars (invented in 1858) were available, and raising agents such as baking soda, baking powder, and packaged yeast had transformed breadmaking and baking. Other ingredients such as cocoa powder, pineapple, cans of salmon, and packaged gelatin began to show up in Ontario cookbooks published in the late 1800s. Local flour, butter, cheese, salt, beer, and liquor were all available. Orchards of fruit trees had been established.

Local grist mills, sugar refineries, and the Goderich salt mine meant that flour, sugar, and salt were much more readily accessible than they had been at the beginning of the century. Still, for both Indigenous Peoples and the early settlers, the growing, producing, preserving, and cooking of food was an all-consuming business.

Not surprisingly, our food reflects our geography: vast and diverse; our history: ancient and modern; and our people: truly and thoroughly multicultural. This book is a mere sampling of Ontario's remarkable culinary landscape and food history.

WHEN BAKING BREAD

Insure
Perfect Results
By using

WHITE SWAN YEAST CAKES

They are the Finest Made by Modern Art and will Make Your Bread Light, White, Sweet and Wholesome.

A Quarter Century Successful Expert Experience Used in Their Manufacture

FORWARD YOUR NAME AND ADDRESS FOR FREE SAMPLE

AT ALL GOOD GROCERS

White Swan Spices and Cereals, Limited
Sole Distributors, Toronto, Ont.

The Relentless Business Of Breadmaking

"Baking [bread] is almost a daily operation," Yorkshire-born Anne Langton wrote in an 1837 letter from her new home in Upper Canada to her brother, William Langton, in England. A year later, in 1838, she recorded a weary note in her diary about "…the eternal almost daily bread-baking."

Making bread was most certainly not an "operation" that Anne Langton would have had a lot of experience with. In her former life she was an accomplished artist and writer, born into a highly cultured, aristocratic family, related on her mother's side to the Brontës. When the family fell upon hard times in England, 33-year-old Anne, her aging parents, and a maiden aunt left their lives in England behind and moved to a rural farm on Sturgeon Lake, near Fenelon Falls, in Upper Canada. The farm belonged to Anne's brother, John, who moved to Upper Canada after he graduated from Cambridge University.

There was little more important to the early settlers than their daily bread. Bread was a staple, life-sustaining food. But the making of bread was no small task. Bread required flour, which, at least until Canadian flour was available, had to be imported and was often either expensive or in short supply, and was especially difficult to obtain for those settlers living away from towns and villages.

(Bottom) Sketch of John Langton's home on Sturgeon Lake, Upper Canada, 1837, by Anne Langton.

Grist for the Mill

Settlers who arrived in Upper Canada from the 1850s on benefitted greatly from the presence of both local wheat and grist mills. Those settlers who came earlier often had to start from the very beginning: clearing the land, planting wheat and other grains, and then harvesting and transporting the grain to the nearest grist mill for grinding. Early grist mills were few and far between. It was not uncommon for farmers to have to travel 50 or 60 miles to the nearest mill.

In addition, right up until the 1850s and beyond, many settlers still had only the open hearth on which to cook. And if all that weren't enough, commercial yeast was not available until 1868, and even then, it was considered something of a luxury. In the meantime, a barm, rising, or starter was required to leaven the dough.

"The usual plan in this country is to mix flour with warm salt and water and set it by the fire to rise. But it must be so carefully watched, the temperature must be kept even, no easy matter in cold weather. Our Mary's method [Mary was a servant to the Langton family] is to boil hops in the water before mixing her rising, and to add a little maple sugar. This has the effect of making the rising keep for a week or ten days... In case of failure there is always a frying-pan cake to resort to, namely, unfermented dough baked in one cake about half an inch thick. I fancy it is bad taste, but I am very fond of these cakes."

"... as for provisions, bread, potatoes, and pork, with the produce of the dairy, are the unfailing ones, but they have been varied here by beef, venison, pigeon pies, and vegetables, of which there are, or may be, plenty in their seasons. There is very little in the way of fruit. John [Anne's brother] has some gooseberry and currant trees planted in his garden. These grow wild in the woods, and of the wild raspberry there is such plenty that they are sold at a shilling a pail... We are too late for these, and for the cranberries too, ..."

Extracts from letters written by Anne Langton to her brother William (in England), shortly after her arrival in Upper Canada in 1837.[4]

Yeast-Making

Before the advent of commercial yeast in 1868, barms, starters, or risings, were created using either potatoes, hops, bran, sugar, salt, rice, milk, pumpkins, or peas. The froth created from brewing beer or distilling liquor, could also be used to rise bread, if one had access to a local brewery or distillery. Starters were treasured possessions and newcomers often relied on their neighbours for their first cup of starter to get their own batch going. Even so, keeping a starter going was challenging in an era before refrigeration in summer or adequate heat in winter.

Simple Starter

Mix two cups of flour with two cups of water, preferably non-chlorinated. Place the mixture in a large well-washed Mason jar, cover loosely, and set the jar on the counter (or someplace warm) where it will capture wild yeast spores from the air. Leave undisturbed for 3-5 days. When bubbles appear on the surface, the starter is ready and can be stored in the refrigerator.

The night before the starter is required, stir the contents of the jar well and remove a cup of the "mother" starter. To the removed starter, add one cup of flour and one cup of warm water. Stir gently and allow this mixture to stand overnight at room temperature, loosely covered. In the morning, the yeast will be ready for use in a bread recipe. Return any leftover starter to the mother starter to feed your starter. Starter should be fed at least monthly. Like most living things, starters can be moody, temperamental, and require maintenance.

A lot of early bread recipes called for cooked potatoes in both the starters and in the bread dough itself. Even after commercial yeast was introduced, many cooks claimed that potatoes added both a silkiness of texture and a smoothness of flavour to bread that could not be achieved any other way.

The recipe below, for "Old-Fashioned Yeast" comes from *The Canadian Family Cook Book*, 1914. It calls for potatoes and hops, and a yeast cake. The introduction of commercial yeast in the late 1860s gradually revolutionized the business of bread-making. But even after commercial yeast became available, cooks adapted slowly, keeping their starters but adding yeast cakes to improve and strengthen the starter. In this way, they could also stretch their use of expensive yeast cakes.

OLD-FASHIONED YEAST

6 large potatoes.
2 qts. water.
½ cup sugar.

½ cup salt.
1 yeast cake.
A handful of hops.

Tie the hops in a piece of cheesecloth and cook in with potatoes. When done put through the colander; add salt and sugar; when luke warm add the dissolved yeast cake; let stand in a warm place, when it will be ready for use; after keep in a cool place. This is excellent and never fails.

THE BLACK BREAD OF SPARTA

Author Susanna (Strickland) Moodie, a member of the literary Strickland family — six of the eight Strickland children became published authors — arrived in Upper Canada in the autumn of 1832. Susanna and her husband, John Dunbar Moodie, and their infant daughter initially settled on a small farm near Cobourg, a long way from Susanna's comfortable early years in Suffolk, England.

Susanna's life in Upper Canada met with a rocky start. When she arrived at her new home, she found a door-less, primitive shack, which housed three young steers, two cows, and a year's worth of manure. The only window had a broken pane of glass. There was no furniture, other than, miraculously enough, a wooden cradle.

Susanna was desperately homesick. The baby cried incessantly. Winter was setting in. Supplies were virtually nonexistent. The neighbours were hostile. To add to the chaos, John Moodie had run into his old friend, Tom Wales, who was both penniless and terribly ill with the ague (a form of malaria), and he brought Tom along to live with the Moodies in their small cabin. The maid, Hannah, promptly absconded. And then, to top it all off, Susanna found herself pregnant.

After she recovered from her initial shock, Susanna took hold of herself and rallied. "When things come to the worst," she wrote "they generally mend." [5]

The Moodie Homes, from *Roughing it In the Bush; Or, Forest Life in Canada*

BAKE KETTLE.

With Deep Rimmed Cover.
9 to 17-in. 4 cents per lb. net.

Bake Kettle from The Chown & Cunningham Catalogue 1890-91

Bran and Vague

As Tom Wales began to recover and gain an appetite, he pleaded with Susanna to make him some proper bread in place of their steady diet of salted meat and bannock, which he called, "the sad bread… the unleavened cakes in the pan."

Susanna acquired some bran and a vague, verbal recipe for how to make bread. She immediately turned her hand to making her first Canadian loaf, though likely it would have been the first loaf of bread she had ever made, anywhere.

She set to making the rising using the bran, a small measure of salt, and enough warm water to make a stiff batter. She placed this into the coffeepot and set it near the fire to ferment. For hours, the bran failed to rise as promised. By morning Susanna found the bran had risen so much it had climbed over the rim of the pot.

She quickly mixed her bread, set her unrisen loaf into the cold bake kettle, and settled it into the fire, then waited impatiently for her first bread, imagining how happy it would make Tom when he arose. "I felt quite proud of it," Susanna wrote, but soon the disagreeable odour of something burning filled the house.

The smell drove Tom from his bed. "Do open the door," he cried, "I feel quite sick!"

Susanna removed the bread from the fire, lifted the lid on her pot and declared the loaf burnt. She placed the charred loaf on the table whereupon Tom stuck a knife in it and then drew it out dripping with raw dough.

"The black bread of Sparta!" Tom said, adding, "Oh Mrs. Moodie, I hope you make better books than bread."[6]

Whigs

Early references to Whigs – slightly sweetened, rich, leavened buns favoured in North West England – date back to the 1600s. The oldest recipes often included caraway seeds or a touch of nutmeg and were typically served with cheese and ale. Whigs were extremely popular in the 19th century, when they were considered a special treat.

The scant two-line recipe for Whigs is exactly as it appears in *The Cook Not Mad* or *Rational Cookery*. (A modernized version of the recipe follows.) Known as Canada's first English-language cookbook, *The Cook Not Mad* was published in Kingston, Upper Canada, in 1831. In fact, it was an almost entirely American book with the most minor of changes. On the cover, for example, the word "American" was replaced with "Canadian."

Whigs or Wigs

One pound flour, four ounces of butter, four ounces of sugar, half a pint of milk, three eggs, tea cup of yeast.

WHIGS

1 cup (or 250 ml) of milk
½ cup (113 g) butter
½ cup (100 g) sugar
½ tsp salt
3/4 cup of starter OR substitute 2 tbsp warm water, plus 1 tsp sugar, and 1 envelope (2 ¼ tsp, or 7 grams) fast-rise yeast
2 eggs, beaten (eggs were smaller in 1831)
4½ cups (520 g) unbleached, all-purpose flour, plus extra for kneading

Scald the milk and add butter, ½ cup sugar, and salt. Let cool to lukewarm. While this is cooling, if using packaged yeast in place of starter, mix together in a separate bowl, the warm water, 1 tsp sugar, and yeast. Let stand.

Add flour to the lukewarm milk and butter mixture and mix well with a wooden spoon. Add the starter or yeast mixture, beaten eggs and stir well. This will make a soft dough but if it is not holding together well enough to turn out and knead, and a little more flour – being careful not to make the dough heavy. Turn out onto a floured surface and knead lightly until the dough looks satiny. Place in a greased pan or bowl in warm spot and let rise until doubled in size.

Once doubled, knead dough lightly again, and shape into small round balls. Place in a greased pan and let rise again, until the buns are doubled in size. Bake at 375 for about 18-20 minutes.

Potato Bread

This recipe for potato bread, simply called 'Bread,' is from *The New Galt Cook Book*, 1898. Note that it calls for one cup of yeast, by which it means one cup of starter.

BREAD.

MISS C. MILLER.

One cup mashed potatoes, one tablespoonful lard or butter, one teaspoonful sugar, one and one-half teaspoonfuls salt, one pint potato water, one pint flour, one cup yeast. Mix the mashed potatoes while hot with the lard, sugar, salt, and the pint of the warm water the potatoes were boiled in, the flour and yeast all together. Beat well for five minutes and leave to rise well covered up. Set this about three in the afternoon (in winter), in the evening add the flour, gradually beating well till too stiff to beat longer, then knead till stiff enough. Keep warm all night. In the morning put into buttered pans, let rise and bake.

As commercial, packaged yeast became the norm, recipes were adapted and mashed potato bread or roll recipes, like the one below, continued to surface in the collections of many home cooks.

POTATO BUNS
1 pkg quick-dry yeast
1 tbsp white sugar
1 cup scalded milk
½ cup sugar
½ cup mashed potatoes
½ tsp salt
½ cup potato water
4 ½ – 5 cups all-purpose flour
1 egg
½ cup margarine [butter]

From *The Alexandra Club Cook Book*, submitted by Mrs. Tillie Brum.

Dissolve yeast in lukewarm water with 1 tbsp sugar and mashed potato.
Add 2 cups of flour. Beat well and let rise ½ hour. Cream butter, sugar, and egg and add to dough. Add remaining flour and salt, gradually.
Add enough flour to make dough stiff enough to handle.
Let rise until doubled in bulk. Shape into buns and let rise again [until doubled]. Bake about 25 minutes at 350°F.

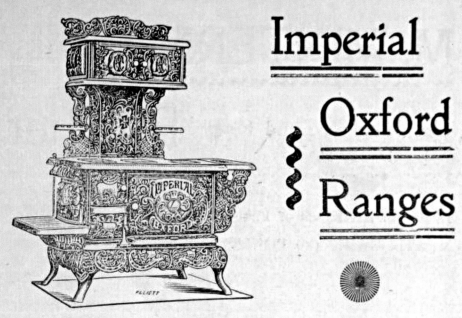

Imperial

Oxford

Ranges

The Oven Ventilation insures Pure and Perfectly
Cooked Foods.

Manufactured by————————

The Gurney Foundry Co., Limited,

OF TORONTO.

————————

Dariel Moulds	Deep Fat Fryer
Border Moulds	Vegetable Slicer
Jelly Moulds	Vegetable Shredder
Ice Plains	Cream Whip
Ice Picks	Universal Food Chopper
Egg Separators	Glass Measuring Cups
Egg Poachers—Steam	Quick Cut Mincers...

FOR SALE BY

❧ HOWIE & FEELY, ❧

Cockshutt Block, Brantford.

MRS. FIFE'S OVERLOOKED ROLE IN AGRICULTURAL HISTORY

The evolution of breadmaking was a long, slow process that sped up dramatically with the industrial revolution. But one of the biggest breakthroughs in breadmaking in North America was agricultural and it started here in Ontario.

Several early wheat crops in Western Canada had failed due to various causes: fighting between the Métis and settlers; lack of knowledge and basic farming equipment; a hurricane in 1817 that levelled the crops; and a grasshopper plague in 1818 that saw billions of the insects devouring every last growing thing from the leaves on the trees to the entirety of the abundant wheat crop. Afterwards, the layers of dead grasshoppers lay inches thick on the ground.

Rust Free

In 1842, David Fife of Otonabee, Canada West (Ontario), planted some wheat seeds on his farm near Peterborough. Amongst the varying stories of how the seeds reached Fife, is an account of an acquaintance of Fife's, who saw wheat seed being unloaded at the Glasgow docks. He gathered a few seeds, put them in his cap, and then sent the seeds to Fife via a friend who was moving to Canada. Fife planted the seeds, now thought to have come from Ukrainian wheat, and that fall he had a small crop of badly rusted wheat, with just five heads that were rust-free.

Fife's wife, Jane (Beckett) was apparently working in the garden when she spotted a cow about to eat the rust-free wheat. She intervened, saved the wheat, and apparently sowed the seeds herself the following spring.[7]

What followed was one of the most successful wheat crops ever planted. Named for the Fife family, Red Fife and its successor, Marquis, developed by Dr. Charles Saunders who crossed Hard Red Calcutta with Red Fife, helped to establish Canada as one of the most important grain producing and exporting nations in the world.

HEINZ
Cream of Tomato SOUP

made with Real Cream

Here is the richness of pure cream, which nourishes, and the appetizing taste of ripe tomatoes, which gives a keener zest to the food that follows.

No artificial thickening or meat stock is used—nothing but tomatoes and real cream. Heinz tomatoes are sun-ripened, and gathered just when they attain their finest flavor.

Heinz Cream of Tomato Soup is perfectly prepared, ready for the table; smooth, rich and tasty. Just heat it. A fine example of Heinz quality.

Some of the 57
Vinegars
Spaghetti
Baked Beans
Tomato Ketchup

All Heinz goods sold in Canada are packed in Canada

HOME COMFORT
VICTORIES

FOUR MEDALS—3 Gold and 1 Silver, World's Centennial Cotton Exposition, New Orleans, 1884.
HIGHEST AWARDS—Nebraska Agricultural Fair, 1887.
DIPLOMA—Alabama Agr'l Society, Montgomery, 1888.
AWARD—Chattahoochee Valley Exposition, Columbus, Ga., 1888.
HIGHEST AWARDS—St. Louis Agricultural and Mechanical Association, 1889.
GOLD MEDALS and 6 DIPLOMAS—World's Columbian Exposition, Chicago, 1893.
HIGHEST AWARDS—Western Fair Association, London, Canada, 1893.
SIX GOLD MEDALS and DIPLOMAS—California Midwinter Fair, 1894.
SILVER MEDAL—Industrial Exposition, Toronto, Canada, 1895.
345,584 Home Comfort Ranges Sold to January 1st, 1897.
☞ Range illustrated sold throughout the United States and the Canadas at a uniform price from our own wagons.
Made of open hearth, cold rolled steel-plate and malleable iron—will last a lifetime with ordinary care.

WROUGHT IRON RANGE CO.,
Founded 1864.   Paid-up Capital, $1,000,000.
Factories, Salesrooms and Offices: ST. LOUIS, MO., and TORONTO, CANADA.
Western Salesrooms and Offices: DENVER, COLO.
☞ We manufacture and carry a complete stock of Hotel Ranges and Kitchen goods; also the unequaled HOME COMFORT STEEL FURNACES. Write for catalogue and prices.

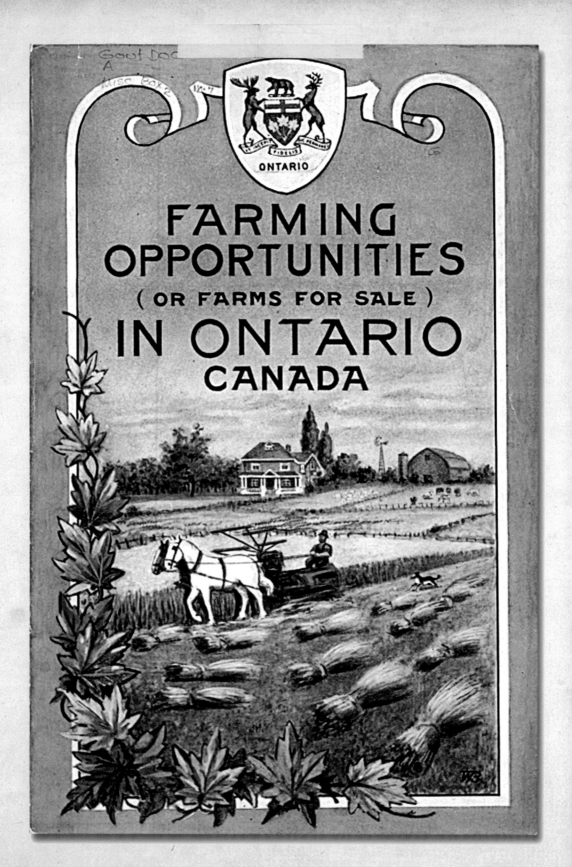

ONTARIO

FARMING OPPORTUNITIES
(OR FARMS FOR SALE)
IN ONTARIO
CANADA

MULTICULTURAL BANNOCK

Bannock (from the Gaelic bannach), is a traditional Scottish quick bread, which was a mainstay of the diet of early explorers, fur traders, voyageurs and settlers to Canada. References to bannock appear in the early journals of the Hudson's Bay Company, which set up posts in Northern Canada in the 1600s. Bannock was prized for its portability and durability which made it a perfect food for travelling.

While it was widely believed that the Scottish introduced bannock to the Indigenous populations, there is plenty of evidence that this was not the case, and that grains including corn flour and the ground roots of other plants were already widely used by various First Nations to make bannock-style breads. What does appear to have been adopted by Indigenous communities is the name itself: bannock.

Later as wheat flour was introduced into the diet of Indigenous populations, its inclusion in bannock recipes became commonplace. Bannock remains an important and immensely popular food with Indigenous populations, where it shows up in many formats, including a much loved and delicious fried version known as "Fry Bread."

The earliest bannocks were small, heavy, flat, dry cakes made with oatmeal, wheat flour, cornmeal, or barley meal, along with water and a little salt, cooked on a griddle over a fire with whatever grease or fat was available. Prior to the 1840s, when both baking soda and baking powder were introduced, bannock was unleavened.

Bannock lends itself well to many variations including the addition of dried fruits like raisins and currants, fresh fruit such as blueberries, buttermilk in place of water, and, once they became available in the mid 1800s, leavening agents.

On the Griddle
Settlers cooked bannock on either a griddle suspended over the fire, or in a cast iron frypan in the bake oven – a small oven that was essentially a hole in the wall next to the hearth, with or without a small door, heated with fireplace stones. From the 1830s on, as wood-fired cast iron stoves became available in Upper Canada, cooking and baking processes were slowly transformed.

Soon after the first Canadian cooking stove was manufactured near Long Point, in Norfolk County, Upper Canada by Joseph Van Nostrand,[8] other stove manufacturers began popping up and stove design evolved from the first short, squat stove to taller, more fashionable, decorative ovens.

Catharine Parr Traill, like her sister Susanna Moodie, wrote about her life as settler in Upper Canada. She warned about bannock: "Careful people, of course, who know this peculiarity, are on the watch, being aware of the ill consequences of heavy bread, or having not bread but bannocks in the house."[9]

Traill's remarks aside, bannock was essential for survival and has a long, important history in both European and Indigenous cultures. Its enduring popularity, particularly amongst Indigenous communities, makes the inclusion of bannock imperative in any discussion of Canadian recipes.

Annie Kadlutikafaaluk boiling water and baking bannock, by Richard Harrington, 1949-1950

Early cookbooks are largely quiet on the topic of bannock, but most offer multitudes of recipes for variations of corn bread, Johnny bread, oatcakes, scones, and galettes – all of which are at least somewhat similar in nature to bannock, that is, portioned, quick breads made from a few simple ingredients.

The Home Cook Book, 1877, lists only one bannock recipe, given here, exactly as it appeared in various versions of the book. These "bannocks" are fried in hot lard, which would make them more like fry bread. Cornmeal was in more common use in the 1800s and contemporary bannock and fry bread are now routinely made with wheat flour.

Bannocks
One pint corn meal, pour on it boiling water to thoroughly wet it. Let it stand a few minutes; add salt and one egg and a little sweet cream, or a tablespoon melted butter. Make into balls and fry in hot lard.

MY MOTHER'S BANNOCK

My mother, Barbara Sutcliffe, who was born in Yorkshire, in 1928, spent her childhood and adolescence living through the aftermath of the First World War, the Great Slump as the Great Depression was known in England, and then the Second World War. In the 1960s, she and my father moved to Canada, with three children in tow, including me – the youngest. From the time she arrived in Ontario, she was extremely interested in First Nations culture, art, pottery, and cooking.

When she was well into her seventies, my mother and two of her female friends, travelled aboard the Polar Bear Express from Cochrane to Moosonee, Ontario. Despite her many travels, this remained one of her favourite journeys.

This recipe came from my mother's recipe collection, though like most home cooks, she didn't note the source. I remember her making bannock and being enthralled with the idea that her recipe for Cree Bannock might easily have been an English scone recipe. She believed that our foods reveal the powerful connections and similarities between all people. In fact, almost every human society around the world has produced some form of a simple unleavened bread by mixing ground grains and water together, for thousands of years.

Barbara Mary Sutcliffe (1928-2017) right, somewhere in the north of England.

Cree Currant or Raisin Bannock

2 cups flour
1 tbsp baking powder
1 tbsp sugar
½ tsp salt
1/3 cup lard or butter
1/2 cup or more of dried currants or raisins
1 cup water

Mix together the flour, baking powder, sugar, and salt. Cut in the lard (or butter) until mixture is crumbly. Then add the currants or raisins and water. Place in a well-greased 8x8 inch square glass pan (or equivalent sized pan of your preference) and bake at 425 for about 24 minutes or until golden brown.

IRISH SODA BREAD

The earliest known soda bread was not made by the Irish, but rather by the Indigenous Peoples of North America who used soda ash (wood ash mixed with water) as a leavening agent for bread.

Pearlash (from potash) and saleratus (potassium bicarbonate) were also used briefly as leavening agents in the early 1800s but were quickly replaced by the introduction of commercial baking soda and baking powder in the mid 1840s. Almost immediately after their introduction, recipes for various "quick breads" such as soda bread began appearing around the world.

Soda bread was particularly important to the Irish, in large part because the introduction of baking soda coincided with the Great Potato Famine of 1845-1849. For the Irish, soda bread was not so much a choice as it was a necessity: a means of putting inexpensive food on the table in a desperate time.

The Irish Arrive

During the Great Famine more than one million Irish died, primarily due to starvation. Another million left Ireland bound for North America. In 1847, ninety thousand Irish emigrants landed in Gros Île before moving on to Quebec City, Montreal, Upper Canada, and the United States.

Toronto's population of twenty thousand temporarily swelled as more than thirty-eight thousand Irish migrants escaping the famine arrived on the city's waterfront – many of them impoverished, hungry and gravely ill. They went on to build lives and communities across the country.

Ontario's two million plus Irish descendants are the largest population of Irish peoples in Canada. Amongst their many contributions, they have given us politicians Edward Blake (second premier of Ontario), Thomas D'Arcy McGee, Sir John Thompson, Brian Mulroney; businessman Timothy Eaton; and suffragist Nellie McClung. And, of course, Irish Soda Bread.

Traditionally soda bread requires only four ingredients: flour, salt, baking soda and buttermilk (or soured milk). Only the quantities vary from recipe to recipe, and even then, only slightly.

Irish soda bread purists object to the addition of other ingredients claiming that adding raisins, currants, sugar, caraway seeds, dried figs, cheese, lemon zest, sugar, or spices will no doubt result in a lovely tea bread or tea cake – but if it's true Irish soda bread that you're after, leave out the extras. Personally, I'm quite fond of raisins in mine, and I'm not averse to including stilton, cheddar, figs, currants, cinnamon or other ingredients either.

This is the standard, ubiquitous soda bread recipe.

Irish Soda Bread

2 cups (8 oz) unbleached, all-purpose flour
½ teaspoon baking soda
½ teaspoon salt
1 cup of buttermilk or soured milk (1 tbsp of white vinegar or lemon juice and then milk to make 1 cup)

Preheat the oven to 400° F. Lightly grease a cake pan.
Combine flour, baking soda, and salt. Add the buttermilk to form a soft, sticky dough..

Place the dough on a floured surface and knead gently.

Shape the dough into a round and place in the cake pan.

With a sharp, wet knife, cut a cross into the top of the loaf.

Bake for approximately 18–20 minutes. Remove from the oven and check for doneness by tapping the bottom of the pan. There should be a hollow sound.

Set the bread to cool on a wire rack.

Bertha Louise (Hearst) White, chopping wood, 7 September 1914.

BERTHA LOUISE WHITE MAKES CORN BREAD

This "Golden Corn Cake" recipe is from the recipe collection of Bertha Louise (Hearst) White, (1886 – 1961). Bertha was born in Arkwright, Ontario, the eighth of nine children. In 1899, when she was 13 years old, her father sold the family farm for 400 dollars and relocated the family to remote Richards Landing on St Joseph Island at the northwestern end of Lake Huron. Bertha's father was John Hearst, the Reeve of Arran Township, and her uncle, William Hearst, became Premier of Ontario in 1914.

On December 26, 1912, Bertha married engineer, Frank Clinton White, and in 1914, she stayed with him in Prince George, BC, where he was designing equipment for a lift bridge on the Fraser River. She kept house in their tent in the lumber camp, gamely sawing and chopping wood. Before long, the couple had five children and in 1923, they moved back across the country.

In 1935, Frank was suddenly taken ill, and at age 46, died on the operating table of the famous neurosurgeon, Wilder Penfield. Bertha was left to raise her five children through the Depression, and still managed to provide them all with post-secondary education. She was renowned as a cook, as well as for her gift of words - as both a religious scholar and a creator of children's verse.

Early settlers in North America were introduced to cornmeal by the Indigenous Peoples, who have used cornmeal for thousands of years, to make various dishes including cornmeal porridge and also a bread known as cornpone (pone from the Algonquin word apan, meaning baked). Without cornmeal, many settlers would have scarcely survived their first harsh years in the New World.

Almost all the cookbooks produced in North America in the 1800s and right up until the mid 1900s listed a variety of recipes for cornbread or corn cake, sometimes known by various names such as Indian bread or Johnny cake (thought perhaps, to derive from "journey" cake). Cornmeal, which was also known as maize or "Indian meal," was used to make cakes, breads, muffins, pancakes, and porridge. Cornmeal was a staple part of the diet until well into the 1900s and continues to be, although perhaps more so in the United States and Mexico than in Canada, where the first fields of wheat grown in Ontario, and later in the prairies, increased the availability of some of the finest wheat in the world.

Cornbread, corn cake, and cornmeal pancakes were a regular feature on the breakfast table of Upper Canadian and early Ontario homes, often served with butter, maple syrup, jam or honey. Cornbread was also served as a savoury dish at lunch, dinner or supper, alongside eggs, beans, bacon, sausages, soup, or stew.

This is Bertha Louise White's Golden Corn Cake recipe.

Golden Corn Cake.

1 cup corn meal.
1 cup flour
1/4 cup sugar
5 teaspoons B. powder

3/4 teaspoon Salt.
1 cup milk
1 egg.
2 tablespoons melted butter.

Mix and sift dry ingredients; add milk, egg well beaten and butter. Bake in shallow buttered pan in hot oven twenty minutes.

PARKER HOUSE ROLLS

There's a longstanding story that in the 1870s an angry cook at the posh Parker House Hotel in Boston, threw a batch of unrisen rolls into the oven, having folded the buns over on themselves so that they approximated the correct height of a fully-risen roll.

The slightly sweet, soft, buttery rolls with their trademark fold became an overnight sensation.

Soon after their inadvertent invention, as if by magic, recipes for Parker House Rolls began appearing in almost every cookbook, all over North America, including remote communities in Ontario. Dora Fairfield of Bath, Ontario, included a recipe in her 1888 book, *Dora's Cook Book*, published by Toronto's Hunter, Rose & Co., and in the 1909, *Culinary Landmarks: Or Half Hours with Sault Ste. Marie Housewives*.

The Toronto Board of Education included a recipe for Parker House Rolls in their 1937 *Handbook of Practical Cookery: For the Use of Household Science Classes in the Public Schools of Toronto*. The recipe continued to crop up in Canadian cookbooks, manuscript cookbooks, and private recipe card collections for decades to come. In fact, nearly 100 years after the initial Parker House rolls incident, the recipe was still appearing in Canadian cook books, including the 1965 version of T*he New Purity Cook Book: A Complete Guide to Canadian Cooking*.

**Parker House Hotel Menu
Cover, January 4, 1858**

ROYAL YEAST CAKES

Parker House Rolls.

1 cup scalded milk.
2 tablespoons butter.
1 tablespoon sugar.
1 saltspoon salt.
$\frac{1}{2}$ Royal Yeast Cake dissolved
in $\frac{1}{4}$ cup lukewarm water.

To the scalded milk add the butter, sugar and salt. Allow it to cool until lukewarm and then add dissolved yeast and 1$\frac{1}{2}$ cups flour. Stir well and let stand in moderately warm place over night. In the morning add enough flour to knead, and let rise until about double in bulk, then roll out $\frac{1}{2}$ inch thick. Cut with biscuit cutter, and brush each piece with melted butter, crease through the centre and fold over. Let rise again until double in bulk and bake for about 25 minutes in moderate oven. Above is sufficient for about ten rolls.

This version comes from the E.W. Gillett Company's *Royal Yeast Bake Book*, 1920.

MOLASSES BROWN BREAD

Until the late 1800s, Canada and the eastern United States were awash in molasses, thanks to trade with the Caribbean sugar industry. Molasses, a by-product created when refining sugar cane or sugar beet into sugar, was considerably less expensive than white sugar, so it was popular in many recipes including gingerbread, biscuits and cookies, brown bread and baked beans. Molasses was also a staple ingredient on many farms, where it was (and still is) sometimes mixed with cattle feed because of its nutritional content. Blackstrap molasses, in particular, is a good source of iron, calcium, magnesium, vitamin B6, and selenium.

Cheap Goods

A note from the 1813 book, *A Geographical View of the Province of Upper Canada and Promiscuous Remarks on the Government*, states: "Dry goods and groceries are brought to Canada, in great quantities, from England and the United States, which, considering the great distance they come, are sold very cheap. At Niagara and other places, green tea is sold for 1 dollar per pound, molasses 10 shillings per gallon, and brown sugar 1 shilling per pound or 8 pounds for a dollar, but since the war [of 1812] it can be had for 8 cents per pound."[10]

This recipe is from the *Purity Flour Cook Book*, 1945.

Molasses Bread

3 cups sifted Purity Flour
¼ tsp salt
1 teaspoon baking soda
½ cup white or brown sugar
1 egg
1 cup milk
1 cup molasses
1 cup chopped walnuts
1 cup raisins

Mix and sift flour, salt, baking soda and sugar. Beat egg and add milk and molasses.

Add liquid to the first mixture.

Add nuts and raisins and mix thoroughly.

Turn into 2 well greased loaf pans and bake in moderate oven (350°F.) for 1 hour.

Proud homeowners, Alex Kouhi and Lempi Koski Kouhi, with three of their children, three more would soon follow. 1929

LEMPI KOSKI'S FINNISH PULLA

Finnish immigration to Ontario began in the late 1800s and continued right through until the 1960s. Finnish-Canadian communities formed right across Canada and in Ontario there were notable populations in Port Arthur (later to become part of Thunder Bay), Toronto, and Sault Ste. Marie. Many Finns were attracted to northern Ontario because of the similarity in climate and conditions, and by the employment and homesteading possibilities.

Sixteen-year-old Lempi Koski was one of those Finnish immigrants. She arrived in remote northern Ontario in 1921, joining her parents and brothers who had arrived a few years earlier and settled in Hearst. Lempi soon found work as a laundress in the tiny railway hamlet of Grant.

The CN Roundhouse
In 1923, with reorganization of the rail lines, Lempi and most of the other inhabitants of Grant, were put on railcars and moved nineteen miles west, to the newly established station railway yard of Nakina, part of the Canadian National Railway. It was in Nakina that Lempi met Alex Kouhi, another Finnish Canadian, and within a year, the two were married. Alex's work in the Nakina CN roundhouse, servicing the large steam engines, kept the pair in the community – a place where they watched their children and grandchildren grow up but were still considered immigrants, decades after their arrival.

This is Lempi's recipe for pulla, a sweet coffee bread flavoured with cardamom, often braided, and essential to Finnish cuisine. The recipe has been adapted by Lempi's granddaughter, Beverly Soloway, who has introduced the bread to two new generations, making this a five-generation Finnish-Canadian recipe.

Grandma Lempi's Pulla

Makes 2 braided loaves
1½ cups warm water
½ cup margarine or butter, melted
2 eggs, beaten
2 packages instant yeast
½ cup white sugar
1 teaspoon salt
2 teaspoons cardamom
6 - 7 cups flour plus more for kneading

Glaze
1 egg combined with 1 tablespoon milk
White sugar for sprinkling

In mixing bowl, combine half of the flour, and all of the yeast, sugar, salt, and cardamom. Mix well. Make a well in the dry ingredients and add the water, melted butter/margarine, and beaten eggs. Stir until combined.
Mix in the remaining flour.
Turn the dough onto a floured surface, and knead for 5 minutes, adding extra flour as needed to prevent sticking. Cover and let rest for 10 minutes. While waiting, grease a cookie sheet large enough to hold two loaves.

Separate dough into 2 pieces. Separate each of these into 3 equal parts. Lightly shape each into a thin rope, about 14 inches long. Using three of the ropes make a braid, pinching the ends together and tucking them under. Put on prepared cookie sheet, placing a strip of parchment paper between the loaves to keep them from sticking together. Let rise for 30 minutes.
Preheat oven to 350°F (175°C).

Before placing in oven, brush the top of the braids with the egg-milk glaze and sprinkle liberally with sugar.

Bake for 35 to 40 minutes. While delicious warm, pulla is even tastier if you wait until it has cooled. Freezes well.

TEA BISCUITS AND SCONES

While bread was imperative for survival, tea biscuits were slightly more luxurious. They were also considered a yardstick by which to measure a cook. Anyone who could create a light, lofty, and flavourful tea biscuit with well defined flaky layers was considered to have the makings of an excellent cook. Tea biscuits were for company – for serving alongside meals. They require deft handling. A little kneading improves the biscuits but too much tends to make them heavy. The dough should be soft and light, not sticky. Tea biscuits do not usually contain sugar, shortening, or other additions.

Scones hail from Britain and unlike their more North American cousins, tea biscuits, they can be either moist or slightly on the dry side, sweet or savoury, patted or rolled out, and often contain additions such as cheese, a little sugar, raisins, currants, chopped dates, crystallized ginger, cranberries, etc. Plain old-fashioned scones are often served with butter, or cream and jam, alongside a pot of tea.

Both recipes are from the *Purity Cook Book*, 1945.

Cream Tea Biscuits

2 cups sifted Purity Flour
4 teaspoons baking powder
1/3 teaspoon salt
3/4 cup heavy sweet cream or 1 cup cream, whipped

Sift together the flour, baking powder, and salt.

Cut in cream to make a soft dough. Turn the dough on to a lightly floured board and knead slightly.

Roll 1/2 to 3/4-inch thick and cut with a floured cutter. Place biscuits on an ungreased baking sheet 1-1 1/2 inches apart if crusty biscuits are desired, otherwise no space need be allowed.

Bake in hot oven (425-450°F or 215-230°C) for 10-15 minutes.

Scones

2 cups sifted Purity Flour
4 teaspoons baking powder
1/2 tsp salt
4 tbsp shortening
1 egg
1/3 cup milk

Mix and sift flour, baking powder and salt.

Cut in shortening with a knife or pastry blender. To well beaten egg add milk and then enough of the first mixture to make a soft dough.

Turn dough out on to lightly floured board and knead slightly. Roll 1/2 – 3/4 inch thick in large rounds. Cut into segments, brush each with milk and sprinkle with sugar and place on a greased baking sheet.

Bake in hot oven (425-450°F or 215-230°C) for 10-15 minutes.

CAKES ON THE GRIDDLE

Bread and potatoes were survival foods for settlers. So what could be better than a crossover between the two? Potato cakes were a favourite of the Irish. They are best served piping hot.

Potato Cakes (below), from *Culinary Landmarks, Sault Ste. Marie*, 1909, submitted by Mrs. J. Dunseath

Potato Cakes

One-quart mashed potatoes, two eggs, a lump of butter size of an egg, three-quarters cup sour milk, a small teaspoon of soda, flour enough to roll, cut in squares. Bake on a buttered griddle or frying pan. When baked brown on both sides, spread with butter, sprinkle a little sugar and put in a covered dish. Very nice.

If potato cakes were a favourite of the Irish, oatcakes were the domain of the Scottish. Oatcakes have been eaten in Scotland since the time of the Roman Conquest of Britain in 43 AD and a mainstay in the Scottish diet for hundreds of years.

English writer Samuel Johnson was rumoured to have said about the Scottish and their penchant for oats, "A grain, which in England is generally given to horses, but in Scotland supports the people." To this, the Scottish Lord Elibank was said to have replied, "Yes, and where else will you see such horses and such men?"

This surprisingly modest recipe (in terms of quantity size) comes from *The Home Cook Book*, 1877. It was submitted by Mrs. J. M. Wetherell. Presumably she was part of a family of three. Also, note that she calls the recipe "Oatmeal Griddle Cakes," but then suggests baking the cakes. Traditionally oatcakes were cooked on a girdle (similar to a griddle but designed to hang over a fire). As ovens became more commonplace, baking also became an option.

Oatcakes are more like biscuits than bread. They are often served with cheese, or butter and jam or honey.

Oatmeal Griddle Cakes

One cup oatmeal, one cup flour, one teaspoon of sugar [1 tablespoon sugar improves the recipe], one teaspoon Cook's Friend baking powder, one-half teaspoon salt; sift the baking powder in with the flour; add cold water to make a batter of the consistency of buckwheat cakes [about ¼ cup of cold water, add more by the teaspoon if required]; beat very well together and bake immediately. [Bake on a greased baking sheet at 350°F for 15–20 minutes.]
This receipt is sufficient for a family of three.

Canuck Rolled Oats advertisement from *The Canadian Grocer*, 1913

BARMBRACK

Barmbrack, barm brack, or simply brack, is a slightly sweet Irish tea bread usually served buttered, along with tea. Typically, barmbrack is studded with raisins that have been soaked in tea, or sometimes tea with a splash of whisky added. It can be made as either a yeast bread or as quick bread with self-raising flour or flour and baking powder. Barmbrack was often served at the Irish festival of Samhain, the precursor of Hallowe'en.

This recipe is from a manuscript cookbook, circa 1840. The author is unknown.

Barm Brack. B. J.

1. egg. 3 or 4 ozs. of butter, 4 ozs. of brown sugar, 3 desert spoon-fuls of carraway seeds, or some currants well picked & washed, or both — The butter to be melted in a cups full of milk & all to be mixed in 3 quarters of a pound of flour, & there added to 1 lb & ½ of dough.

(Page 43, top) Nasmiths Bread Delivery Wagon, Earlscourt, Toronto, 1907

Barmbrack　　**from a family recipe**

1 ½ cups of raisins (or raisins and currants mixed)
½ cup sliced red glace cherries (have used dried cranberries when out of cherries)
1 cup cold, strong black tea
¼ cup whisky
1 cooking apple, peeled and grated or finely chopped
¾ cup light brown sugar
2 cups unbleached all-purpose flour
3 tsp baking powder
½ tsp salt
½ tsp each ground cloves, nutmeg, ginger
1 egg, beaten

Soak the raisins, currants, and cherries in the cold tea and whisky overnight.

Generously butter a 1-pound loaf tin (or round cake tin) and set oven temperature to 350°F.

Add all remaining ingredients to fruit/tea mixture and stir to mix. The dough will be very stiff. Place the dough in prepared pan and bake for 45-50 minutes. Check for doneness and cook another 10-15 minutes as required.

Cool in the pan and turn out when fully cool. Improves if you wait 24 hours to eat but can be eaten right away. Outstanding sliced thinly and served with butter and honey.

Bkt
BECKERT'S
GARDEN FIELD AND FLOWER
Seeds
1903
W.G. BECKERT, ALLEGHENY, PA.

ALL SOUP IS GOOD FOR THE SOUL

Soup is known in almost every culture around the world and has been since the first clay cooking pots were made, at least twenty thousand years ago.

For thousands of years before the Europeans first arrived in North America, Indigenous Peoples had been making soups and stews from foods indigenous to the continent including corn, beans, and various squashes. These foods were introduced to the settlers by Indigenous Peoples and soon became staples in their diets as well.

A soup known as sagamité to the French Canadians and onnontara to the Iroquois, was made daily according to Jesuit missionary Father Joseph Francois Lafitau, who wrote in 1724, "Every morning the women prepare this sagamité for the nourishment of the family."[11] Other early French explorers also referenced the soup, which was made from cornmeal cooked in water and sometimes included dried fish, beans, meat, squash, or berries.

Keep it Simmering

For settlers, soup was as fundamental as bread, potatoes, and salted meat. A soup or stew pot, kept simmering on the hearth or over the fire, provided a method of temporarily preserving food safely and keeping harmful bacteria at bay. Fish and animal bones and vegetable scraps and peelings were boiled down to make stock, which provided vital nutrients, reduced waste, and provided a base for soups, stews, and gravy.

It was not uncommon to keep a pot of stock or soup simmering for a couple of days. Leftovers, which could not simply be consigned to a refrigerator or freezer as they are today, were added to stock to make soups.

For those early Canadians living from the land, soup was often served as a meal, augmented by bread. In town and for the upper classes, soup was served as a course, typically at dinner. Formal dinners in the 1800s consisted of at least three courses and when company was invited, there could be twelve or more courses. As a rule, the wealthier one was, the later and longer they dined. Either way, on the land or in town, early dinner or late, every proper formal meal began with soup.

THE THREE SISTERS

Corn, beans, and squash – collectively known as the Three Sisters – were staples of all North American Indigenous agriculture. The plants, when grown together, support each other, just like good sisters.

Corn stalks provide a pole for beans to grow on, while squash grow under the shade provided by the bean plants. The beans provide nitrogen for the corn and squash, and the leaves of the squash and pumpkins keep the moisture in the earth from drying out, thereby conserving water for all three plants. Grown together in this way, the three plants form a neat little ecosystem. When the vegetables are cooked together, they provide a balance of carbohydrates, protein, fibre, and vitamins.

First Nations and Metis cultures have an oral tradition for passing on knowledge from generation to generation. As such, written recipes have not traditionally been part of the culture. What is possibly the earliest recorded "recipe" for Three Sisters Soup came from William Clark, in a December 23, 1804, entry to the *Journals of the Lewis and Clark Expedition*:

> ```
> "She made a Kettle of boild Simmins pumpkins, beens, Corn,
> & Choke Cherris with the Stones, which was paletable
> considered as a treat"
> ```
[12]

The reference to "Simmins" has sometimes been translated to persimmons. But in an earlier journal entry, made on December 5, 1804, Clark was clear: "simmins" were pumpkins: "Several Indians also visited us," he wrote. "One brought Pumpkins or Simmins as a present, a little Snow fell in the evening at which time the wind Shifted round to N. E."

Three Sisters Soup adapted from the reference made by William Clark on December 23, 1804.

Three Sisters Soup

2 tbsp butter or olive oil
1 small onion, finely chopped
2 cups corn kernels cut from the cob (or use canned or frozen)
1 ½ cups of cooked cannellini beans, (if using canned beans, rinse thoroughly)
4 cups of butternut squash, peeled and cubed
4 cups stock
Salt and pepper and ½ tsp dried sage

In a large soup pot, sauté the onion in the butter or olive oil. Add the corn, beans, squash, and stock. Simmer until the vegetables are tender, adding more stock or water only if needed. Mash gently. Season generously with salt, and pepper and stir in the sage. Ladle in bowls and top with a small knob of butter. Serve with bannock.

RUB-A-BOO – A SOUP OR STEW

Rubaboo or rababoo was a catchall name for a soup, stew, or porridge eaten primarily by the Métis, the coureurs de boi and voyageurs. It was often made by boiling pemmican and water, and then thickening the mixture with flour. Other versions included rabbits, peas, corn, turnips, and bear or pork grease, all boiled together to form a thick stew.

This version from *The Canadian Economist*, 1881, requires two pounds of pemmican.

Mr. J.W. Wardope, who sent the recipe in, noted wryly, "This is an exceedingly nice dish for those who can spare the time to take about sixteen hours vigorous exercise after eating it."

TO MAKE RUB-A-BOO.

Mr. J. W. Wardrope, Winnipeg.

Take about two pounds of pemmican and chop it up very fine. Put it in an iron pot, cover with water, and let it boil for about two hours. Then stir in enough flour to make a *very* thick soup. Serve hot on tin plates. This is an exceedingly nice dish for those who can spare the time to take about sixteen hours' vigorous exercise after eating it.

A Note About Pemmican

For well over two centuries, beginning in the late 1500s, the fur trade was the economic engine that fuelled the exploration and growth of Canada. The main staple of the fur trade was beaver, the pelts used primarily to meet a nearly insatiable demand by Europeans for beaver-felt hats.

In 1670, the Hudson's Bay Company (HBC) was incorporated by British Royal charter. Once the world's largest landowner, the Company owned Rupert's Land - nearly four million square kilometres of territory in the Hudson Bay watershed. HBC functioned as a de facto government, trading post, supplier, and controller of the fur trade. Indigenous Peoples were critical to the fur trade; they did all the trapping and without their manpower, expertise, and the pelts they delivered, the fur trade would never have existed.

The early fur trade fuelled Canada and in turn the fur traders were fuelled by pemmican. Introduced by Indigenous Peoples, pemmican, from the Cree word, pimikân, quickly became a staple food of the early explorers and fur traders. Made from pounded dried meat (traditionally bison, though moose, elk, venison, caribou and eventually beef were also used); grease or melted fat; and dried fruits such as blueberries, cranberries, currants, juniper berries, or chokeberries, packed into leather pouches sealed with grease – pemmican made an ideal, potent, portable travel food: long-lasting, filling, and high in calories and protein.

POTATO SOUP

This recipe for Potato Soup from *The Home Cook Book*, 1877, requires that the cook start by boiling a shank of beef for two days. This made perfect sense in an era when homes were heated by fireplaces and pots could be left simmering over the hearth. It makes a lot less sense today. But for those lucky enough to have both a wood-fired stove and three days to make a pot of potato soup, (if not, substitute any good stock) here is the recipe as it first appeared as one rather long, run-on sentence:

Potato Soup

Boil a shank of beef two days before you want your soup, strain into a crock, and let stand until you need it, the fat will rise to the top, this you must take off before beginning to make your soup, now take your soup pot and in about two tablespoons of the same fat, fry brown four large onions sliced, put in half your stock, have ready a pot of nicely mashed potatoes, stir the potatoes into the soup till about the thickness of thick cream, and season with pepper and salt. The remaining stock is valuable for graveys, &c., or Scotch Broth instead of mutton.

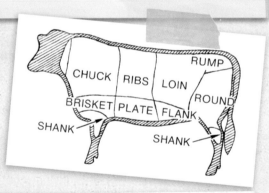

(Below) By 1914, a much easier version of potato soup appeared in *The Canadian Family Cook Book: a volume of tested, tried, and proven recipes.*

POTATO SOUP

One carrot, one onion, two large potatoes chopped fine. Boil, and put through a colander; then add pepper and salt to taste; add a good sized piece of butter, and one quart of milk; let come to a boil and serve.

CURRY AND THE BRITISH RAJ

Mulligatawny is the English interpretation of an originally vegetarian Indian soup that originated in Madras. The British were in India from the mid 1700s until 1947, and during that time, many Indian dishes and flavours made their way into the British diet, albeit with adjustments, such as the addition of chicken or other meat to mulligatawny.

Mulligatawny was a fashionable soup throughout the 1800s and well into the 1900s but was especially popular during the years of the British Raj – that is – the rule of the British Crown over India from 1858-1947.

Many early Canadian cookbooks include recipes for "India Pickles," chutneys, dal, mulligatawny and various curried dishes, such as curried chicken. The British used the term curry to refer to both the collection of spices that typically make up curry powder and spicy dishes in general. Curry powder was in common usage in Upper Canada almost as soon as the British arrived. In an August 1839 diary entry, Anne Langton wrote, "Pickling has been the order of the day. We consume more in the ways of ketchups, sauces, curry powder, etc. than we used to at home, on account of the many months we are without fresh meat."

Mulligatawny

Fry one cup of uncooked minced chicken until brown. Also brown one-fourth cup each of carrot, onion, and celery, diced and one finely chopped green pepper, one sliced apple, mix, add one-third cup of flour, one teaspoon of curry powder, a blade of mace, two cloves, one cup of tomatoes and simmer all for an hour. Strain, press the vegetables through the sieve. Add five cups of white soup stock, pepper and salt; sprinkle minced parsley over the top and serve with boiled rice.

(Above) from The Family Herald Cook Book, 1924.

(Right) Map of "British India" 1880.

THE POWERHOUSE SCOTS

Between 1783 and 1855, more than one-hundred thousand Scottish emigrants settled in Upper Canada. Throughout the 1800s and early 1900s, the Scots banded together to become a collective powerhouse in Upper Canada and throughout the emerging nation of Canada. From the beginning they were highly entrepreneurial, hardworking, hard living, active in building key infrastructure, and played leading roles in the social, political, and financial landscape of the country. As of the 2011 Census of Canada, Scottish Canadians were the third largest ethnic group in the country.

Clan Fraser Dinner

When Colonel Alexander Fraser, publisher, historian, founder of the 48th Highlanders Regiment, and later, the Archivist of Ontario, helped to organize the first annual Clan Fraser Dinner, in Toronto, in May 1894, the first course, hardly surprisingly, was Scotch Broth.

Scotch Broth shows up in many early cookbooks in various formats, mostly requiring a neck or leg of mutton. When lamb or mutton were hard to come by, a beef shank was substituted. A couple of bone-in lamb or mutton chops could also easily be substituted.

The main ingredients of Scotch Broth are typically lamb, mutton, or beef; barley; root vegetables such as carrots, turnips, swedes (or rutabagas); and sometimes leeks, cabbage, and dried beans or peas.

Scotch Broth adapted from *The Magic Cook Book*, 1930

Scotch Broth

4 quarts (8 cups) water
2 lbs neck of mutton (lean)
½ cup barley
1 onion, 1 small turnip, 1 rutabaga, 1 carrot, all peeled and chopped
Plenty of salt and pepper

Wash the mutton. Wash and drain the barley.

Bring the water to the boil in the soup kettle. When it boils,

add the meat and boil hard for five minutes. Draw from the fire and add barley.

Place on fire again and boil slowly for one hour.

Add the onion, turnip, rutabaga, and carrot. Cook altogether for 45 minutes, then remove the meat from the pot, (discard the bone), trim and chop the meat and return it to the pot.

Season with salt and pepper.

"MOR FHAICH"

CLAN FRASER
IN CANADA,
FIRST
ANNUAL DINNER
MAY 5TH
1894

Clan Fraser in Canada First Annual Dinner, May 5, 1894 – menu cover and menu.

A chuirm sgaoilte ; chuasai an ceol
Ard sholai a'n talla nan triath.—OISEAN.

Menu

Soup.
Scotch Broth.

Fish.
Boiled Sea Salmon from the Cruives of Lovat.
Sgadan beag Poll-a-Roid.
Pomme Natural, Anchovy Sauce.
Bread and Butter Rolled.

Entrees.
HAGGIS
PUNCH A LA ROMAIN.

Joints.
Roast Beef.   Spring Lamb.

Vegetables.
Mashed Potatoes.
Asparagus.   French Peas.

Entremets.
Curds and Cream.   Fraser Pudding.
Shortbread.   Oat Cakes.
Cheese.   Biscuits.   Assorted Fine Cakes.
Neapolitan Ice Cream.   Nuts.   Figs.   Radishes.
                                              Dates.
FRUITS.   COFFEE.

51

MOCK TURTLES AND OTHER MOCK THINGS

Mock turtle soup was one of a number of 'mock' dishes that became popular in the late 1700s, a trend that continued until well into the 1900s. The mock goose recipe that appeared in 1747, in The Art of Cookery, Made Plain and Easy, by Hannah Glasse, may have been the forerunner for other mock dishes including mock chicken pie, mock oyster and turtle soups, mock mincemeat, mock cream, and mock cherry pie.

Hannah Glasse's Mock Goose recipe was simple: "Some love the knuckle [of Pork] stuffed with onion and sage shred small, with a little pepper and salt, gravy and apple-sauce to it. This they call a Mock-Goose."

Most mock foods were invented out of necessity, either because the main ingredient was so popular it had become too expensive (goose and poultry in general) or just outright depleted (oysters and turtles), or because the ingredients were difficult to find, such as cherries in Upper Canada before orchards were planted. Cranberries mixed with raisins substituted for cherries. Pork was a frequent substitution for chicken because pork was much less expensive during the Victorian era.

In the case of turtles, the immense desirability of turtle soup, driven by its popularity in British royal households, caused a turtle shortage. Green turtles, in particular, were hunted to near extinction. Mock turtle soup was the result. So famous was the soup, that Lewis Carroll wrote about it in Alice's Adventures in Wonderland.

> "Then the Queen left off, quite out of breath, and said to Alice,
> 'Have you seen the Mock Turtle yet?'
> 'No,' said Alice. 'I don't even know what a Mock Turtle is.'
> 'It's the thing Mock Turtle Soup is made from,' said the Queen."

Most early recipes for Mock Turtle Soup called for a calf's head, a commodity that is increasingly difficult to come by. This recipe calls instead for a soup bone and a quart of turtle beans, both of which can be found at most major Canadian supermarkets. Ask the butcher for a large beef bone or just substitute stock. Also, start with a small (rather than large) spoonful of powdered cloves and add more if required. Once you get past the black colour of the soup, it is quite mild and surprisingly delicious.

Mock Turtle Soup from *The Home Cook Book*, 1877

Mock Turtle Soup
One soup-bone, one quart of turtle beans, one large spoonful of powdered cloves, salt and pepper. Soak the beans overnight, put them on with the soup-bone in nearly six quarts of water and cook five or six hours. When half done, add the cloves, salt and pepper; when done, strain through a colander, pressing the pulp of the beans through to make the desired thickness [some beans could be left whole], and serve with a few slices of hard-boiled egg and lemon sliced very thin. The turtle beans are black and can only be obtained from large grocers.

ELIZABETH POSTHUMA SIMCOE AND COLONEL PICKERING'S SALMON CHOWDER

The year was 1791. Twenty-five-year-old English artist, writer, and heiress Elizabeth Posthuma (Gwillim) Simcoe was setting sail from England along with her husband, Colonel John Graves Simcoe, who was on his way to take up his post as the first Lieutenant Governor of Upper Canada. The couple had their two youngest children in tow, two-year-old Sophia and son Francis, aged three months. Four older daughters (the oldest of whom was only seven) were left behind in England for the five years their parents would be away.

An orphan from birth (her mother had died while delivering her and her father had died before she was born), Elizabeth was given the middle name Posthuma by her mother's sister in recognition of the sad circumstances of her birth. Elizabeth was christened the same day her mother was buried. Raised in an upper-class English family, Elizabeth was the heiress to a great fortune. By the time she was 16 years old she was married to John Graves Simcoe.

Elizabeth Posthuma (Gwillim) Simcoe

Life in the Colony

Despite the fact that Elizabeth Simcoe had lived a life of privilege and wealth that included servants and nurses; ball gowns, parties, and elaborate dinners; and a formal education in music, art, language and literature, she flourished in Canada and threw herself fully and admirably into life in the colony, never complaining, unfailingly buoyant. She was surprisingly open-minded and egalitarian.

She loved her five years in Upper Canada. At the time, Upper Canada was still little more than a vast forest inhabited by a mere ten thousand settlers, many of them Loyalists who were primarily living along the main southern waterways. The Indigenous population was not yet accounted for.

The Simcoes lived for a time in Niagara before moving to York (now Toronto). John Graves was often away travelling and attending to his duties as Lieutenant Governor, leaving Mrs. Simcoe to fend for herself in the "canvas house" they called home. While in Niagara, in January 1793, Elizabeth Simcoe gave birth to her seventh child, a daughter named Katharine. A little over a year later, in April 1794, Katharine was buried in York.

Elizabeth Simcoe's sketches, letters, and diary (published as The Diary of Mrs. John Graves Simcoe, Wife of the First Lieutenant-Governor of the province of Upper Canada, 1792-6) are amongst the most important records of life in the earliest days of the province.

Elizabeth revelled in adventure. She participated in all that Canada had to offer. She admired and respected Indigenous Peoples, desperately wanted to ride in a canoe, was amused by sled dogs, delighted in leaping her horse over logs, loved a party, spoke French whenever possible, constantly searched out new vistas and scenes to sketch and paint, and kept herself busy with her friends, her family, and her diary.

Snakes in a Barrel

She was fascinated with the wildlife and deeply curious about rattlesnakes, whose presence she wrote about over and over. So deep was her interest in the snakes that she once received a gift of two live rattlesnakes delivered in a barrel.

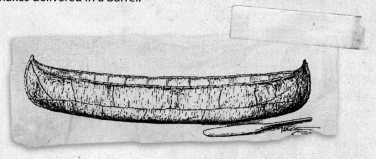

She collected native remedies and recorded Indigenous words in her diary. She wrote endlessly about the food.

Even the death of her seventh child could not defeat her. Her only complaint was not the cold, or the isolation, or the time away from her four older children, or of missing her homeland, or about the tent-home in which she lived; but on occasion, she objected to the heat and humidity of summer, which caused her to suffer. Hardly surprising when one considers that she came from the cool, green, damp north of England.

Elizabeth felt that her son Francis (for whom Castle Frank in Toronto was named) had a special connection with Indigenous people. He was apparently frequently rude to guests but was unfailingly well-mannered to any Indigenous visitors. She wrote about the politeness of the Indigenous visitors, who brought gifts including a much-treasured beaver blanket for the governor's bed. Captain Joseph Brant, leader of the Mohawks, was a guest of the Simcoe's during their stay in Niagara.

Elizabeth Simcoe was Besotted with Canoes

"To see a Birch Canoe managed with that inexpressible ease & composure which is the characteristic of an Indian is the prettiest sight imaginable," she wrote. "A man usually paddles at one end of it & a woman at the other but in smooth water little exertion is wanting & they sit quietly as if to take in the air. The Canoe appears to move as if by clockwork. I always wish to conduct a Canoe myself when I see them manage it with such dexterity & grace. A European usually looks awkward & in a bustle compared with the Indian's quiet skill in a Canoe."

Perch and Venison

On March 19, 1796, she wrote, "We dined in the Woods on Major Shanks' farm Lot where an arbour of Hemlock Pine was prepared, a band of Music stationed near. We dined on Perch & Venison. Jacob the Mohawk was there. He danced Scotch Reels with more grace & ease than any person I ever saw & had the air of a Prince. The picturesque way in which he wore & held a black blanket, gave it the air of a Spanish Cloak, his leggings were scarlet, and on his Head & arms silver bands. I never saw so handsome a figure."

But perhaps the best contributions of Mrs. Simcoe's diary were her extensive references to food. En route from Quebec to her new home in Upper Canada, on December 2, 1791, she recalled eating "… part of a metiffe, a bird between a wild goose (the outarde) [Canada Goose] & a tame one. It was much better than a tame Goose."

Moose Lips

She dined on mouffle (moose lips); "It is a very rich dish with an excellent sauce;" on toasted thin slices of venison cooked on sticks over the campfire; on wild ducks fed on wild rice, which she claimed were better than any she had ever tasted; and "Some small Tortoises cut and & dressed like Oysters in Scollop [sic] Shells were very good at Supper." For afters there were all manner of cakes, sweets, and nutmeats.

There was often venison, wild turkey, wild goose, partridge, pigeons, and other small birds and animals on the menu. "The black Squirrel is large & quite black," she wrote. "It is as good to eat as a young rabbit." And on November 20, 1793, "We dined in the Woods & eat part of a Raccoon, it was very fat & tasted like lamb if eaten with Mint sauce."

Simcoe's journal contains a multitude of references to fruit – cherries, wild gooseberries that "when they were stewed found them excellent sauce for Salmon," peaches, hurtleberries, bilberries, "Punkins," strawberry spinach [rhubarb], wild grapes, "the finest red watermelons," and apples both fresh and dried, especially the "excellent Apples called Roseaux, pink throughout… a flavour of strawberries." She collected May Apple seeds to send back home to England with instructions, she gathered butternuts, and she bought maple sugar and birch sap vinegar from Indigenous Peoples.

"The Indians bring us cranberries in Spring & Autumn which are as large as Cherries & very good, the best grow under water," she wrote. "They also supply us with Chestnuts which they roast in a manner that makes them particularly good." She also learned Indigenous remedies such as calamus root for cough, sassafras root for the ague, and sweet marjoram tea for headaches. In time she learned about Wintergreen and Ginseng, and other local plants, such as consumption vine, sore-throat weed, and Dewberry's Wild Turnip.

There was an abundance of fish through all the seasons including winter: salmon, sturgeon, pickerel, "Maskalonge (a superior kind of Pike)," as well as trout, and whitefish.

"We have had a great many whitefish. They are caught here from October till April. In summer they go into deeper water; they are most exquisitely good & we all think them better than any other fresh or salt water fish, they are so rich that sauce is seldom eaten with them, but it is a richness that never tires it is of so delicate a kind. They are usually boiled or set before the fire in a pan with a few Spoonfuls of water & an anchovy which is a very good way of dressing them."

MASCALONGE.—*Lucius Masquinongy.*

On June 26, 1793, she wrote, "Coll. Pickering gave me a receipt [recipe] to make Chowder of Salmon, Sea biscuit & pork; it is to be stewed for twenty minutes." On October 28, 1793, she wrote, "Today we walked 2 miles to a pretty spot by the side of a creek where we had a fire made of many large Trees & wild ducks roasted by it & we dined without feeling the least cold. Coll Pickering's Dish, chowder, is also easily dressed in the Woods, being prepared in a Kettle before we left our house."

Sadly, Mrs. Simcoe did not record the salmon chowder recipe in her diary, though this "Fish Chowder" recipe, from *The Toronto Cook Book*, 1915, certainly resembles the one that Colonel Pickering suggested. Just like Colonel Pickering's recipe, it calls for fish, crackers (sea biscuit), and pork, with the addition of potatoes – all ingredients available from ship' provisions.

The recipe gives the typically ambiguous advice to, "Use only enough cold water to moisten and cook." Depending on the amount of water one added, this could more of a stew, or a scallop, or even a contemporary casserole, than a soup. Bacon would make a reasonable substitution for salt pork.

Fish Chowder

Quarter pound salt pork, three medium sized potatoes, one and a half pounds fish, quarter of a pound crackers or biscuits. Cleanse, remove the rind and cut the pork into thin slices; slice the onions. Put the pork and onions together into a pot and fry them brown; then season lightly with salt and plenty of pepper. Slice the potatoes and lay them in cold water until wanted. Scrape, cleanse and wash the fish; cut it into small pieces; soak the crackers in water or milk until tender. When the pork and onions have browned and been seasoned, add a layer of fish; on the fish a layer of potatoes; on the potatoes a layer of crackers; then repeat the process, commencing with fish, in regular layers until the pot is nearly full, or till the ingredients are used up. Each layer is seasoned with pepper and salt. Use only enough cold water to moisten and cook. Cover the pot closely, set it over a gentle fire, let it heat gradually, and cook and serve. Tomatoes may be added as one of the layers.

MAD FOR OYSTERS

Oysters were cheap, plentiful, and almost ridiculously fashionable through the 1800s and early 1900s. Shop owners, hoteliers, and tavern keepers went to great lengths to keep oysters on hand year-round. Oysters were packed live in barrels and transported by boat and stagecoach before rail lines existed. During the winter months, supplies of oysters were buried in beds of damp sand mixed with cornmeal and routinely watered.

Oysters were popular dinner party fare. A note in *The Home Cook Book*, advises, "The order of wines is sometimes perplexing, and the novice should remember that Chablis or Sauterne comes with the small oysters before soup, and that sherry is drank after soup."

And a paragraph or two later: "…a guest draws off his gloves, and lays them in his lap under the napkin, which should be spread lightly not tucked in the dress. The raw oysters are eaten with a fork; the soup, only a ladleful to each plate, is sipped from the side of the spoon, without noise, or tilting the plate."

Used in soups, stews, and curries, oysters were also served raw, fried, broiled, boiled, pickled, creamed, escalloped, skewered, and fricasseed, and they were made into patties, croquettes, fritters, and pies. Oyster soup was practically mandatory at New Year's Day levees and formal gala dinners.

Oyster Soup

2 tbsp soda biscuit crumbs
1 tbsp butter
1 cup milk
8 or 10 oysters
¼ tsp salt, few grains of pepper

Scald the milk in a saucepan, adding the cracker crumbs and seasonings.

Then add the butter and oysters. When butter is melted, the oysters are done.

Oyster Soup from the *Handbook of Practical Cookery: Household Science Classes in the Public Schools of Toronto*, 1937. Makes two small servings.

Beer and Oysters

Oysters were so lauded that they were ascribed with healing properties and often prescribed to the sick. In her diary, the young Sophia MacNab, living in Dundurn Castle in Hamilton, wrote about her ailing mother's propensity for oysters, which she often ate for lunch with beer. On Friday January 23rd, 1846, Sophia reported that her mother had eaten nine oysters and a half tumbler of beer for lunch. In the next entry, she wrote, "I came in and made myself neat, after that I went to see Mamma and she ate six Oysters and some beer…"[13]

Oysters had long been a food source for Indigenous Peoples but by the 1920s, the North American love affair with oysters was such that the eastern oyster beds were beginning to be depleted. Now recognized for their role in water purification, wild oysters are being re-introduced to ancient oyster beds around the world.

SOUP KITCHENS OF THE GREAT DEPRESSION

Canada was among the nations most severely impacted by the Great Depression from 1929-1939. After the stock market crash of 1929, sales of commodities such as wheat, lumber, and paper dried up. Almost nobody in Canada was exempt from the effects. Millions of Canadians were unemployed and hungry, and many were homeless.

A drought in the prairies exacerbated the problem. By 1932, Canada experienced a 34.8 percent decline in per capita gross domestic product. Food was a significant issue for almost everyone. And when President Herbert Hoover introduced new tariffs on imports to the United States, the Canadian economy went into complete freefall.

Breadlines and Soup Kitchens

Some families lived for days on little but bread and a bit of molasses, or bread and lard. Elsewhere people were eating squirrels, gophers, and ketchup soup. Or a steady diet of potatoes. Or puffed wheat.

Scurvy and other dietary deficiency diseases become common. Roast beef was replaced by casseroles and meatloaf, and for those even less fortunate: soup. Breadlines, relief camps, and soup kitchens were the new reality. Towns became famous for their soup kitchens. The town of Port Arthur's[14] was said to be the best in the country.[15] Soup saved many from starvation. Those who could, helped those that could not. Spontaneous soup kitchens popped up everywhere – in church

Food Lineups during the Great Depression, Yonge Street Mission, Toronto, 1930s

halls, in out-of-use warehouses, community centres and even family homes. Pea soup, once the dish of French-Canadian millworkers, became the standard fare of soup kitchens. Hearty, filling, and inexpensive, it could also be kept going on the stove for days on end and watered down to feed extra bodies as required.

Pea soup is usually made with stock, most often made from boiling down a ham bone. This version from *The Canadian Economist* simply required water. Soups like this one helped keep the nation alive through the Depression.

PEA SOUP.

Mrs. James Cunningham, Ottawa.

One quart of split peas, boiled in three quarts of water until quite soft. Then drain it through a colander. Toast a slice of bread and cut it up into small pieces, and fry the same until quite brown in a greased pan, add this to the soup with a quarter pound of butter, and pepper and salt to taste.

PAULINE JOHNSON: GIFTED POET AND CRACKERJACK COOK

The year was 1861 and Canada was marching towards confederation when Emily Pauline Johnson Tekahionwake (meaning 'double wampum' or double-life) was born on the Six Nations Reserve near Brantford, Upper Canada. She was the youngest child of English-born Emily Susanna Howells and Mohawk Chief George H.M. Johnson (Teyonhehkon).

Pauline Johnson grew up knowing both her ancestral cultures. By the time she was a young adult, she was a published writer and much sought-after speaker. She spent her life smashing gracefully through gender and race barriers.

Her Indigenous heritage was a prominent theme in her writing. Her love of canoeing, for example, was illustrated in her famous poem, "The Song My Paddle Sings." The loss of love was another of her great themes. Pauline's poet friend, Charles Mair, said of her writing, "The defeat of love runs like a grey thread through much of Miss Johnson's verse."[16]

Pauline Johnson Tekahionwake 1895, by Charles Scriber Cochran.

Pauline Johnson graced stages throughout Canada, the U.S., and England, giving poetry recitals to adoring audiences. After nineteen trips crisscrossing Canada on the newly built Canadian Pacific Railway, she eventually moved to Vancouver, where she entertained frequently and generously. She once wrote in a letter to her friend Archie Morton, "Did you even know that I am a crackerjack of a cook?"[17] Another friend said that Pauline, "was more genuinely pleased with a delighted remark over a grilled steak, a perfectly roasted chicken, or a beautifully assembled salad than she was over a compliment paid to a new poem."[18]

When Pauline Johnson died of breast cancer on March 7, 1913, days shy of her 52nd birthday, obituaries ran in newspapers across the nation, public offices were closed, flags were flown at half-mast, and wreathes were sent by the Prime Minister and Governor General. Pauline was remembered for her Indigenous heritage, her talents, her gift for friendship, and her legendary kindness. William Arthur Deacon said in Toronto's Saturday Night, "Canada means a little more because Pauline Johnson lived and wrote in it."[19] The nation had lost a beloved daughter.

The Corn Husker
By E. Pauline Johnson

Hard by the Indian lodges, where the bush
Breaks in a clearing, through ill-fashioned fields,
She comes to labour, when the first still hush
Of autumn follows large and recent yields.

Age in her fingers, hunger in her face,
Her shoulders stooped with weight of work and years,
But rich in tawny colouring of her race,
She comes a-field to strip the purple ears.

And all her thoughts are with the days gone by,
Ere might's injustice banished from their lands
Her people, that to-day unheeded lie,
Like the dead husks that rustle through her hands.[20]

THE IMPORTANCE OF CORN

Corn, potatoes, tomatoes, squash, and cocoa all originated in the Americas – and all became part of the Columbian exchange – that is, the transfer of people, plants, animals, diseases, and technologies between the New and Old Worlds, thought to have begun with Christopher Columbus in 1492. It was, for example, the British explorer, Sir Walter Raleigh (1552-1618) who, in 1589, transplanted the first potatoes to his home near Cork, Ireland. And it was the Spanish Conquistadors who in the 1500s transplanted the first tomatoes from Peru to Europe; and brought turkeys from Mexico to Spain.

No discussion on North American agriculture would be complete without mentioning the importance of corn (also known as maize), which was first domesticated by Indigenous Peoples in Mexico about ten thousand years ago. Corn found its way around the world, eventually becoming the biggest grain crop produced on the planet.

The Corn Maize

Maize has been grown in what is now Ontario for at least fifteen hundred years by the Haudenosaunee Confederacy, also known as the People of the Longhouse, Iroquois, or Six Nations (Mohawk, Oneida, Onondaga, Cayuga, Seneca, and Tuscarora nations); and at least five hundred years ago the Huron Wendat had an estimated twenty-three thousand acres of corn under cultivation.[21]

Corn was critical to the survival of the First Peoples of North America, who in turn taught the settlers to grow and use the crop. Maize was and is used to make a wide variety of foods including breads, cakes, pancakes, soups, stews (such as succotash), porridge, grits, salads, and popcorn, and it can also be eaten straight off the cob.

The relationship between corn and humans is symbiotic. Maize is entirely dependent on humans for propagation. Conversely, corn is such a massive food and fuel source globally that were there to be a widespread corn crop failure the results would be catastrophic. Quite simply, corn is fundamental.

Corn Fritters

from *The Alexandra Club Cook Book*, 1952, submitted by Mrs. C.N. Cockburn

1 can corn, drained
2 eggs, well-beaten
1 tsp sugar
2 tsp baking powder
1 cup flour
½ tsp salt
¼ tsp paprika

[Mix all ingredients together.] Batter should drop from a spoon as for pancakes. Cook in a little hot fat, like pancakes.

SORREL

Common sorrel, also known as garden sorrel, is a much-overlooked perennial herb that has been cultivated for centuries. Sorrel can be used in salads, soups, sauces, quiches, frittatas, and almost any recipe calling for spinach or other dark leafy greens. Sorrel is at its best in spring and early summer, when the leaves are still young and tender.

Sorrel is remarkably easy to grow, though surprisingly difficult to buy or find in North America. It overwinters well, even in Ontario, and once established is generally one of the first greens to make an appearance in the garden each spring. Colewort (in the recipe below) is a leafy green from the Brassica family. Collard greens, kale, or arugula could all be substituted.

Dreers Garden Catalogue page showing sorrel and others, 1884

From *The Canadian Economist*, 1881

Sorrel Salad

Take young, tender colewort plants, sorrel lettuce, endive, celery, parsley, full-grown onions, which are better to cut and eat in winter, and season them with salt, cream, and vinegar; add sugar if approved.

DORA FAIRFIELD MAKES SALADS

Dora E. Fairfield, a member of a prominent Loyalist family who settled in the small village of Bath, near Kingston, was 26 years old and single when her 311-page cookbook, *Dora's Cook Book*, was published by Hunter, Rose and Co. in 1888. She included recipes for all the standard fare of the day: Roast Goose, Potted Pigeon, Curried Chicken, Stewed Squirrels, Port Wine Sauce for Game, Salmon Salad, Watercress Salad, Scrambled Eggs, Scalloped Frogs, Cabbage Salad, Burnt Butter [Sauce] For Fish, Corn Meal Flapjacks, and Charlotte Russe.

Dora's simple, attractive, and delicious red salad with an oil-and-red-vinegar dressing is a gem of a recipe.

Red Salad

Boil small red potatoes in their skins; when cool peel and slice them a little thicker than a penny. Some of the inner part of a red cabbage must be sliced as thin as possible; mix equal parts of potato, [red] cabbage, and beet root boiled. The dressing must be [olive] oil poured over, salt, pepper, and red vinegar.

Watercress Salad

Watercresses as a salad are best served simply with a sauce of lemon juice and olive oil poured over them in a salad bowl.

Pineapple Salad

Pare a large pineapple and dig out the eyes; then with a silver fork, tear the fruit downwards into shreds until all is removed from the core. Put the shredded fruit into a dish, sift with powdered sugar and pour over it the juice of two good oranges, or pour over it a little port wine and a dash of brandy.

(Top) Red Salad from *Dora's Cook Book*, 1888

(Left middle) Watercress Salad from *Dora's Cook Book*, 1888

(Right middle) Pineapple Salad from *Dora's Cook Book*, 1888
[N.B – you will need a very ripe pineapple and also, according to Dora, a silver fork.]

THE TENACIOUS, PRACTICAL, AND PROLIFIC DANDELION

Common dandelions (*Taraxacum officinale*) were brought to North America in the mid-1600s by the first European settlers. The plant promptly seeded itself everywhere, growing in places where almost nothing else would grow.

Settlers used every part of the plant for food, wine, beer, and medicinal purposes. The vitamin-packed young dandelion leaves are amongst the first greens of spring, and are excellent used in salads, along with other greens like mustard greens, chickweed, lamb's quarters, watercress, and spinach. Older dandelion leaves can be boiled and used like cooked spinach. The flowers were used to make wine and dye for fabrics and wool.

When resourceful English settler Susanna Moodie fell upon hard times in Upper Canada and could no longer afford the luxuries of tea and sugar, she discovered that by washing, drying, roasting, and grinding dandelion roots, she could produce her own passable coffee substitute. With time she learned that dandelion roots collected in the autumn made better coffee than those collected in the spring. "The result," Susanna wrote, in *Roughing it in the Bush*, "was beyond my expectations. The coffee proved excellent – far superior to the common coffee we procured at the stores."

Dandelion Salad [Two Ways] from the *Blue Ribbon and Pure Gold Cook Book*, 1905

Dandelion Salad

1. Gather only the freshly-grown plants. The tender leaves make an excellent salad with bacon dressing (see below).

2. The whole [dandelion] plant, after thoroughly washing, may be boiled until tender, drained, chopped fine, seasoned with salt, vinegar and butter. Those who think it too bitter may use half spinach or beet leaves.

Bacon Dressing
4 slices of bacon, well cooked and crumbled or finely chopped, reserve bacon fat and keep warm
1 tsp of sugar
¼ cup cider vinegar
Salt and pepper to taste
Add the sugar and cider vinegar to about 2 tbsp of the warm bacon fat, along with the crumbled bacon. Add salt and pepper to taste. Serve with dandelion salad.

[Cooked] Mayonnaise Dressing from the *Coburg Congregational Cook Book*, 1909
Beat 3 eggs, 1 tablespoon of butter, 1 teaspoon dry mustard, ½ cup vinegar, a salt spoon of salt, quarter cup of sugar, pinch of Cayenne pepper. Cook in double boiler as you would custard. – Miss Martha Field.

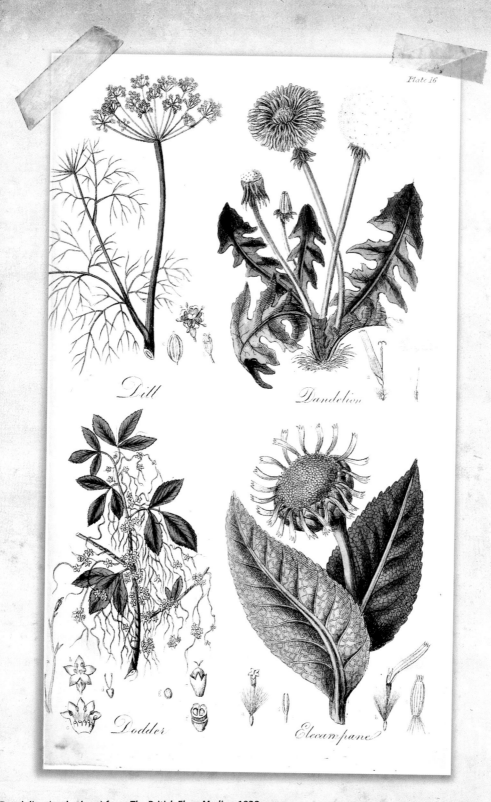

Plate 16

Dill

Dandelion

Dodder

Elecampane

Dandelion (and others) from *The British Flora Medica*, 1838.

VEGETABLE DISHES

With the exception of salad, which would have only been available during the warmer months, vegetables were almost always served cooked in the 1800s. Celery was often braised and cucumbers were stewed. In her 1888 book, Dora Fairfield included a recipe for "Scalded Lettuce," which included washed and dried lettuce leaves fried in pork drippings with salt and pepper, then doused in a cup of vinegar and simmered.

Dora also listed cooking times for vegetables that suggested cooking carrots, string beans, parsnips, spinach, or cauliflower for one to two hours; dandelions (she didn't specify which part of the dandelion) for an astonishing two to three hours; and then, curiously, recommended boiling potatoes for only 30 minutes.

Here, just for fun, is an unbelievably complicated recipe for cooking cucumbers from *The Canadian Agriculturist*, 1856.

Stewed Cucumbers

Take two or three straight cucumbers, cut off one end, then take out the seeds, lay them in vinegar and water, and pepper and salt; have some good farce [stuffing], and fill each cucumber with it; dry your cucumbers well out of the vinegar first, then dry them in a clean rubber; then fry them, if for brown; if for white, not; take them out of the butter, and put them to stew in some good stock, with one onion, a fagot of herbs, a slice of lean ham, until tender; thicken the liquor, and pass through a tammy [a flat sieve]; season with a little drop of vinegar, lemon juice, sugar, salt, and white pepper; glaze the cucumber several times to a light brown.

Egg Plant

Pare and cut into slices one-quarter inch thick. Sprinkle slices with salt. Lay on plate and place weight on to express juice. Leave one hour. Drain, dip in batter of egg and crumbs, sauté in butter or bacon fat until brown.

Egg Plant from the *Handbook of Practical Cookery: Household Science Classes in the Public Schools of Toronto*, 1937

Yam Puff

4 large yams or sweet potatoes
¼ cup butter
2 well beaten eggs
¼ cup sugar
2 tsp baking powder
1 tsp salt

Peel sweet potatoes and boil until soft. Mash and add the remaining ingredients. Beat well and put in a buttered casserole dish. Dot with butter, and bake until brown and about half an hour or more in a moderate oven (350°F).

PARSNIP FRITTERS.

Scrape and boil tender, two large parsnips, rub through a colander and mash. Beat in 1 egg, 2 tablespoons of milk, two teaspoons of flour, one half teaspoon of salt, one fourth teaspoon of pepper. Make into small flat cakes, flour slightly and fry in butter or good dripping. Brown on both sides,—Eva Battell

Salsify

Salsify, like parsnip, is another member of the dandelion family. Salsify was particularly popular with the Victorians, in part because it is said to have a faint taste of oysters, but also because this is a vegetable that stores well over winter. Rich in umami flavour, salsify is making a well-deserved comeback. It can be roasted, boiled, sautéed, or mashed and used in soups and stews.

Salsify

Scour, pare, cut into inch lengths. Drop into cold water with one teaspoonful of vinegar. Cook in boiling water until tender (15–20 minutes). Add salt after first 10 minutes. Serve with a [thickened white] sauce made with milk and some water in which salsify has been cooked.

(Top) Yam Puff adapted slightly from the *Opti-Mrs Cookbook*, 1950, submitted by Mrs. Frank Archer

(Middle) Parsnip Fritters from the *Coburg Congregational Cook Book*, 1909

(Bottom) Salsify from the *Handbook of Practical Cookery: Household Science Classes in the Public School of Toronto*, 1937

THE SWEET BEET

Beetroots, or beets as they are typically known in North America, are a justifiably popular vegetable. They are relatively easy to grow, delicious, store well, are excellent served hot or cold, can be pickled, and are excellent in soup such as borscht.

In 1747, Professor Andreas S. Marggraf, a physicist at the Academy of Science in Berlin, discovered that beetroots could be converted to sugar. And unlike sugar cane, beets grow well in temperate climates such as Canada. By 1902, Ontario had four sugar-beet manufacturing plants in operation.

Though the etymology of the name Harvard Beets is unclear (some claim a Harvard University student invented the dish, others say the dish originated at a pub that was either called Harwood or located in the suburb of Manchester known as Harwood) the dish itself is quite universal. It consists of chopped or sliced, cooked beets served in a sweet vinegar sauce, thickened with cornstarch. A recipe for Harvard Beets appeared in the 1911 edition of *The Boston Cooking-School Cook Book* by Fannie Farmer Merritt. By the 1930s, Harvard Beets were appearing every-where, including in the dining cars of the Canadian Pacific Railway.[22]

Harvard Beets from *The Boston Cooking-School Cook Book*, 1911

Harvard Beets

Wash twelve small beets, cook in boiling water until soft, remove skins, and cut beets in thin slices, small cubes, or fancy shapes, using French vegetable cutter. Mix one-half cup sugar and one-half tablespoon corn-starch. Add one-half cup vinegar and let boil five minutes. Pour over beets, and let stand on back of range one-half hour. Just before serving add two tablespoons butter.

LATKES

According to the 1871 Census (the first official Canadian census post Confederation), there were 1,115 Jewish people in Canada, most of them in Montreal, but smaller Jewish populations lived in Toronto, Hamilton, and other communities around the new country. The first synagogue in Toronto was established in 1856. By the outbreak of the First World War, there were an estimated one hundred thousand Jewish Canadians, mostly living in Montreal and Toronto.

Jewish cuisine was shaped by the widespread dispersion of the Jewish community throughout the world. Some dishes, however, have become fairly consistent favourites such as borscht, challah, bagels, babka, blintzes, beef brisket, smoked salmon or lox, gefilte fish, variations of chicken soup, stuffed cabbage rolls, honey cake, apple cake, and of course, latkes, which are often associated with Hanukkah.

The first known reference to latkes at Hanukkah came from Rabbi Kalonymus ben Kalonymus, (c. 1286-1328) who was raised in Provence but living in Italy when he mentioned latkes in a poem about Hanukkah. He was referring to little Italian pancakes made with ricotta. Potato latkes are a much more recent invention that sprang from a series of crop failures in Eastern Europe in the 1800s, which resulted in widespread planting and use of potatoes.

Potato Latkes

2 ½ lbs russet potatoes, peeled whole and submerged in ice cold water
1 large onion, finely diced
2 large eggs, beaten
1 tsp kosher salt and a good grind of black pepper
½ cup vegetable oil such as corn oil - more may be required
Sour cream to serve

Peel the potatoes and submerge in a large bowl of ice water. Grate the potatoes into a large mixing bowl, working quickly to avoid having the potatoes brown. (If you use a food processor, be careful not to turn the potatoes to mush by over-processing.)

When the potatoes are grated or processed, place in a colander and press firmly to release all the water. The drier the potatoes, the better. If you're in doubt, dump the grated potatoes onto a clean tea towel and roll the potatoes in the towel to remove any remaining liquid.

Place the grated potatoes in a mixing bowl and add the beaten eggs, salt, and black pepper.

Heat about half the oil in a large non-stick frypan. Once the oil is hot, using a large serving spoon, scoop the batter into the hot fat being careful not to crowd the pan. Allow the latkes to cook about two or three minutes each side to make sure the potato is cooked properly.

Remove the browned latkes to cookie sheets (again being careful not to overcrowd) and place in a warm oven until the latkes are ready to serve.

BAKED BEANS

Haricot beans, also known as navy beans – the legume typically used to make baked beans – originated in South America and were first imported to Europe in the early 1500s. The French used the beans to make cassoulet – a slow-cooked stew of beans, duck or goose confit, and meat usually including sausages - that was the likely precursor of modern day baked beans.

By the mid-1800s, baked beans were a standard food item for the American Navy, hence the emergence of the term navy bean. Around the same time, versions of baked beans, with subtle regional differences, cropped up throughout the United Kingdom and Ireland, Europe, Australia and New Zealand, and throughout North America. The inclusion of a small piece of salt pork in many North American canned beans is in part because of the importance and prevalence of salt pork in the diets of early settlers.

Add Maple Syrup

Baked beans were and are popular throughout Canada, but were especially popular among French Canadians, who often sweetened the beans with maple syrup. The French, and later French-Canadian, presence is a tremendously important part of Ontario's history. The land now known as southern Ontario and southern Quebec was part of the first "Province of Quebec." It wasn't until 1791 that the land was divided into Upper and Lower Canada.

The first settlements in what is now Ontario, including those in the Detroit-Windsor area, Sainte-Marie among the Hurons in Midland, and Sault Ste. Marie, were all French settlements dating back to the 1600s. Even after 1791, French-Canadian settlements in Ontario continued to be, and remain, an important part of the province's economic, cultural and culinary history, with more than six hundred thousand Franco-Ontarians making their home here.

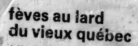

fèves au lard du vieux québec

1 lb de fèves blanches ST-ARNAUD
½ lb de lard salé
½ tasse de mélasse
¼ de tasse de cassonade
1 c. à thé de moutarde sèche
1 c. à thé de sel
¼ de c. à thé de poivre noir
2 ou 3 oignons, hachés

Rincer et faire tremper les fèves recouvertes d'eau toute une nuit. Les faire bouillir dans la même eau 15 à 30 minutes. Mêler les ingrédients secs et la mélasse dans une tasse à mesurer, ajouter de l'eau et mélanger. Mettre les fèves dans un pot de grès de 4 lb, ajouter le mélange de mélasse et recouvrir d'eau. Ébouillanter et gratter le porc salé, couper en petits morceaux. Disperser le porc salé et les oignons dans les fèves. Couvrir et mettre au four à 250°F de 7 à 8 heures. Ajouter si nécessaire de l'eau bouillante au cours de la cuisson pour couvrir les fèves. Enlever le couvercle 2 heures avant la fin de la cuisson pour faire brunir les fèves. (7 à 8 portions)

This recipe for baked beans comes from the kitchen of Marie Thérèse Levasseur Pépin (1923 – 1995). It was taped to the lime-green Tupperware container in which she always stored her dried beans. Since her recipe did not call for maple syrup, Thérèse's seven children were allowed to pour their own maple syrup directly on their baked beans, making this meal a much beloved family favourite.

It is that real oven-baked flavour that has made

HEINZ Baked Beans

the choice of people everywhere. And they have that flavour because they are really oven-baked— as the label states.

MADE IN CANADA
AT LEAMINGTON · ONTARIO

ONE OF THE
57
VARIETIES

HEINZ
BAKED BEANS
WITH PORK AND
TOMATO SAUCE
HEINZ

Heinz Baked Beans label, Leamington, ON, circa 1910.

Baked Beans of old Quebec (translated from French version)
1 lb white [navy] beans
½ lb salt pork [or bacon]
½ cup molasses
¼ cup brown sugar
1 tsp dry mustard
1 tsp salt
¼ tsp black pepper
2 or 3 onions, chopped

Rinse the beans, and soak all night covering them with water. Boil the beans in the same water [changing the water is usually recommended in contemporary recipes] for 15 to 30 minutes.

Mix all dry ingredients and the molasses in a cup and add water to mix. Put the beans in a 4-lb clay bean pot, add the molasses mixture and cover all with water. Scald and scrape the salt pork, cut in small pieces. Spread the salted pork and the onions amongst the beans. Cover and cook in the oven at 250°F for 7 to 8 hours. Take the lid off two hours before the end of baking to brown the beans. Makes 7-8 servings.

"DOESN'T FALL" CARROT SOUFFLÉ

This recipe comes from the collection of
Ruth Marian (White) Redmond, 1919 – 2016,
daughter of Bertha Louise (Hearst) White,
1886 – 1961, whose Golden Corn Cake
recipe appears earlier.

Ruth was born in Chatham, Ontario, the only
girl amongst four sons born to Bertha and
Frank White. At age 16, she attended McGill
University, where she received her Bachelor
of Arts Degree and teaching diploma. After
several years of teaching and a year of selling books at the Eaton's Department Store
in Winnipeg, she returned to McGill to do
her Bachelor of Library Science degree.

While back in Montreal, Ruth met and
married Donald Redmond. They moved
to Nova Scotia and then with three small
children in tow, moved abroad and in
lived in Ceylon, Turkey, and Kansas before
returning to Kingston, Ontario, where Ruth
lived and cooked, until she died at age 96
in 2016.

Ruth Marian White, age 5, 1924.

Gallons of Soup

Ruth was fascinated by cookbooks and food preparation. Growing up during the Great Depression,
she learned not to waste. She was a generous cook though, always making wonderful meals for her
children and extended family, routinely baking bread and cooking gallons of soup.

In the 70s, Ruth was the chief buyer and cook for Meals on Wheels in Kingston. Though she was a
great believer in sharing food and recipes, her carrot soufflé recipe was the one recipe she kept to
herself, believing that every good cook needed an ace up their sleeve. This carrot soufflé was
Ruth's ace.

Despite the fact that Ruth Redmond called this a soufflé recipe, the egg whites are not beaten
separately, making this more akin to a savoury carrot pudding than a soufflé. "Doesn't fall," Ruth
scrawled, assuredly, on her handwritten recipe, adding, "Even people who don't like carrots usually
love this."

Carrot Soufflé

2 cups cooked carrots, puréed
1 tsp salt
¼ cup liquid honey
1 ¼ cups rich milk or thin cream
3 tbsp cornstarch
3 eggs, well-beaten
4 tbsp melted butter

Stir into puréed carrots the salt, honey, and milk with cornstarch dissolved in it. Then add the well-beaten eggs and last, the melted butter. Pour into a buttered casserole dish and bake 45 minutes at 400°F. (Done when table knife inserted in the centre comes out clean.)
Serves 6-8

(Right) Varieties of Carrots: D.M. Ferry Seed Annual, 1916.

DANVERS   CARROTS   CHANTENAY

GUERANDE OR OX HEART

IMPROVED LONG ORANGE

CHEESE.

1—Gorgonzola. 2—Double Gloucester. 3—Koboko. 4—Parmesan. 5—Dutch. 6—Roquefort. 7—Schabzieger. 8—Dunragit. 9—York Cream. 10—Port du Salut. 11—Cheddar. 12—Pommel. 13—Camembert. 14—Mainzer. 15—Cheshire. 16—Stilton. 17—Cream Bondon. 18—Gruyère. 19—Wiltshire Loaf. 20—Cheddar Loaf.

THE BIG CHEESE

The Big Cheese en route from Ingersoll to England via the New York State Fair, 1866

Cheesemaking began in Canada in the early 1600s with the arrival of Samuel de Champlain and the first cattle. As more settlers slowly began to arrive, bringing with them more cattle, those living on the land who could afford a cow or two began to make their own cheese. Imported cheese remained an expensive commodity.

It wasn't until 1864, when American entrepreneur Harvey Farrington convinced Upper Canada's Oxford County farm women to quit making their own cheese and sell him the milk instead, that the first Canadian cheese factory, The Pioneer, was established in Norwich.

Other factories quickly followed suit. By 1866, three local Oxford County cheesemakers hatched a plan to garner attention for both their cheese and the newly minted Ingersoll Cheese Manufacturing Company of Oxford, by making a 7,300-lb (3,311-kg) wheel of cheddar. The cheese cured for three months in a specially built shed and in August 1866, the Big Cheese was transported to the train station in Ingersoll on a wagon pulled by six horses.

An Industry is Born
The cheddar was exhibited at the New York State Fair in Saratoga before heading to England, where it was purchased by a Liverpool merchant. The Big Cheese helped establish Oxford County as the birthplace of Canada's commercial cheese industry.

The Giant Cheese was a huge commercial success and suddenly there was a big demand for Canadian cheddar. By 1867, Ontario had gone from having a small handful of cheese factories to having more than 200, with many dairy operations churning out butter as well. Exports of cheese, primarily to England, had become a significant part of Canada's early economy.

The Big Cheeses

But competition was fierce and promotion was vital. Another massive cheese project was needed. This time the cheddar was made in Perth, Ontario. The 22,000-lb (9,979-kg) mammoth cheese was displayed at the Chicago World's Fair before, like its predecessor, being shipped to England. In short order, Ontario had become famous for its world-class cheese.

Ontario's big cheeses had not only captured the imagination of the world, but also inspired James McIntyre's 1884 poem, "Ode on the Mammoth Cheese Weighing Over 7,000 Pounds" - widely considered to be one of the worst and yet most enduring (and cheesiest) poems in Canadian history

The poet, 24-year-old James McIntyre, left Scotland and arrived in Upper Canada in 1851, and promptly found work as a hired hand. A few years later, McIntyre moved to Ingersoll, where he became an undertaker and ran a furniture store that sold, among other things, pianos and coffins. In his spare time, he dabbled in poetry and eventually became known as Canada's "cheese poet." McIntyre is the inspiration for Ingersoll's annual cheese-themed poetry competition, held to this day, in his honour.

Mammoth Cheese leaving Perth en route to the World's Exposition at Chicago, April 1893

By 1900, spurred on by all the province's cheesemaking success, there were 1,242 cheddar factories in Ontario and cheddar had become Canada's second-largest export, behind timber. Exports of Canadian dairy products, especially to England, continued through the 1900s, especially during the war years when Britain needed Canadian food supplies desperately.

Sadly, in 1952, after almost a century of encouraging and requiring Canadian dairy imports, Britain shut down the importing of all Canadian cheddar, forcing more than 100 Canadian cheddar factories (mostly in Ontario) to close down.

(Left) "Ode on the Mammoth Cheese Weighing Over 7,000 Pounds" by James McIntyre[23]

(Bottom) 1893 Mammoth Cheese Poster

Ode on the Mammoth Cheese

We have seen the Queen of cheese,
Laying quietly at your ease,
Gently fanned by evening breeze
Thy fair form no flies dare seize.

All gaily dressed soon you'll go
To the great Provincial Show,
To be admired by many a beau
In the city of Toronto.

Cows numerous as a swarm of bees
Or as the leaves upon the trees
It did require to make thee please,
And stand unrivalled Queen of Cheese.

May you not receive a scar as
We have heard that Mr. Harris
Intends to send you off as far as
The great World's show at Paris.

Of the youth -- beware of these
For some of them might rudely squeeze
And bite your cheek; then songs or glees
We could not sing o' Queen of Cheese.

We'rt thou suspended from baloon,
You'd caste a shade, even at noon;
Folks would think it was the moon
About to fall and crush them soon.

1893 **1893**

THE MAMMOTH CHEESE

THE MAMMOTH CHEESE WAS MADE AT THE

DOMINION EXPERIMENTAL DAIRY STATION

AT PERTH, LANARK COUNTY, ONTARIO.

It is going to form part of the Pyramid of CANADIAN DAIRY PRODUCTS at the World's Columbian Exposition at Chicago

207,200 pounds of Milk were used in making it; that quantity is equal to the milk, for one day in September, of 10,000 cows.

The CHEESE WEIGHS 22,000 Pounds

It is incased in a mould or hoop of steel boiler plate, 5-16 of an inch thick, and a pressure of more than 200 tons was applied to make it perfectly solid.

IT MEASURES 28 FT. IN CIRCUMFERENCE BY 6 FT. IN HEIGHT.

The Canadian Pacific Railway Company will run a special World's Fair Cheese Train Leaving Perth at 7.00 a.m. on MONDAY, APRIL 17th, 1893.

A SPECIAL TRUCK Has been made for transporting the MAMMOTH CHEESE through Great Britain after it leaves Chicago.

STARTERS AND LIGHT SUPPERS

Appetizers or Hors d'oeuvres (the latter translating to "outside of the work") first began appearing in upper class homes in Britain and North America in the mid to late 1800s. By the turn of the 20th century, both terms were cropping up on formal menus. Early appetizers were most often simple dishes that preceded the soup course, and might include olives, nuts, oysters, devilled eggs, and canapes such as caviar on toast.

Even though the recipe below for cheese straws suggests that they might be "very nice with salad," these cheesy pastries would be even nicer served with a cocktail before dinner. The recipe predates the cocktail party – a concept which took hold in the 1920s.

Cheese Straws from *The Toronto Cook Book*, 1915

Cheese Straws

One cup of flour, two cups chopped cheese, one tablespoon butter, pinch of salt, one scant teaspoon baking powder, mix with water and roll out like pie crust, cut in strips and bake a light brown. This is very nice with salad.

Soufflés

Soufflés got their start in France in the early 1700s and take their name from the French verb souffler, which means to blow, puff, or inflate. Sweet or savoury, soufflés depend on the air in the beaten egg whites for volume.

Cheese Soufflé

Cheese Soufflé from the *Purity Cook Book* (1945 revised edition)

2 tbsp butter
3 tbsp Purity flour [or any all-purpose flour]
½ tsp salt
½ tsp dry mustard
1/8 tsp pepper
½ cup scalded milk [heated to just under boiling point]
1 cup grated cheese [extra sharp old cheddar or gruyere]
3 eggs separated

Melt the butter and blend in the flour, salt and pepper [and ½ tsp dry mustard]. Add scalded milk gradually, mixing thoroughly. Pour into top of double boiler and cook over hot water with constant stirring until mixture thickens. Add cheese and stir until it is melted. Beat egg yolks with a fork until they are light and creamy. [Add a little of the sauce to the egg yolk mixture and mix thoroughly, then add this mixture to the remainder of the sauce.] Mix well and cool. [In a clean dry bowl, with clean beaters] beat egg whites until stiff and fold into cheese mixture. Turn into a greased [soufflé] dish [or individual ramekins] and bake in a moderate (350° F) oven until firm.

WELSH RAREBIT

Welsh Rarebit, also known as Welsh Rabbit, is a glorified but delicious version of cheese on toast. The dish has been known by both terms since the 1700s.

Whether to call it a rabbit or a rarebit seems to be the subject of considerable debate and contention. According to Fowler's 1926 *Dictionary of Modern English Usage*: "Welsh Rabbit is amusing and right. Welsh Rarebit is stupid and wrong." That may be so, but I'm going to stick by the name I've known since childhood: Welsh Rarebit.

In the first edition of *Mrs. Beeton's Book of Household Management in 1861*, Mrs. Beeton referred to the dish as Welsh Rare-bit.

In the 1912 edition of her book, renamed *Mrs. Beeton's Cookery Book*, published several years after her death, the issue of which name was correct, was neatly side-stepped and the dish was entitled as follows:

Welsh Rabbit or Rarebit

4 oz of Cheshire or Cheddar cheese [about one cup of grated cheese]
½ oz [1 tbsp] of butter
2 or 3 tbsp of milk or ale
Mustard
Pepper
Buttered toast

Cut [grate] the cheese into small pieces, place these in saucepan with butter, milk or ale, ½ a mustard-spoonful of mustard [¼ tsp of dry mustard] and pepper to taste and stir the mixture by the side of the fire until it resembles thick cream. Have ready some squares of hot well-buttered toast, pour on the cheese preparation and serve at once.

THE RABBIT.

MAC AND CHEESE

Mac and cheese has been around for more than six hundred years. An early recipe appeared in the 14th-century English cookbook, *The Forme of Cury*, which featured a dish called makerouns made of pasta layered with melted butter and cheese.

In 1802, American President Thomas Jefferson, who had eaten macaroni in Europe, served a baked macaroni pie at an American state dinner, setting off a North American love affair with macaroni and cheese. Recipes for macaroni pies soon followed, popping up in cookbooks including Mrs. Nourse's, *Modern Practical Cookery*, published in Montreal in 1845. Mrs. Nourse lived in Edinburgh but played an important role in Canadian culinary history when her comprehensive cookbook became the third English-language cookbook published in Canada.

To Dress Macaroni, with Cheese from Mrs. Nourse's Modern Practical Cookery, 1845
For a large dish, take half a pound of macaroni; stew it in water, with a little salt, until tender, drain it, return it to the pan, with a little cream, let it stew until it is rich and thick; season with beaten mace, a teaspoonful of made mustard, mixed with two spoonful of cream, and the yolks of two raw eggs beat up; add the eggs and cream, give it a toss; have a dish ready lined with puff paste, pour in the macaroni; grate Parmesan or Cheshire cheese over it; bake in a moderate oven.

During the 1800s, pasta, in the form of either macaroni or vermicelli, was one of the very few convenience foods available. Vermicelli was typically used in soups. Macaroni, which came in the form of long tubes, was used to make savoury baked dishes.

An anonymous note in *The Canadian Agriculturist*, 1848, reads, "I had a box of macaroni in the closet, that most valuable viand, which no country house keeper should ever be without, if she can possibly procure it, so acceptable at all times, and particularly valuable for an emergency…"

KD is Born

James Lewis Kraft, who built an empire based on processed cheese and macaroni, was born on a dairy farm near Stevensville, Ontario in 1874, to Mennonite parents, George and Minerva Krafft (the second 'f' in the surname was eventually dropped). The young J.L. Kraft grew up delivering dairy products, including cheese, from a horse-drawn wagon in Fort Erie, Ontario.

In 1903, recognizing the bigger market south of the border, Kraft moved to the United States with 65 dollars in his pocket and his horse, Paddy. Four of his brothers soon joined him and in 1914 the Kraft Brothers opened their first cheese manufacturing plant.

By 1916, J.L. Kraft had patented a process for pasteurizing cheese so that it would resist spoiling. A couple of decades later, in 1937, Kraft Foods Inc. released their new product, "Kraft Dinner," in the United States and Canada. KD, as it soon became known in Canada, was marketed with the slogan, "A meal for four in nine minutes for an everyday price of 19 cents." The timing of the product release, during the Great Depression, could not have been better. Kraft Foods Group Incorporated is now widely recognized as the second largest food company in the world. Not bad work for a boy from Stevensville, Ontario.

HANNAH JARVIS ON HOW TO STORE EGGS WITHOUT A REFRIGERATOR

Before barns or hen houses were heated, egg production often slowed down in winter, making eggs a relatively scarce commodity. Preserving eggs was useful, particularly for the winter months but also during the fairer weather to prevent eggs from being wasted during an egg glut.

Writer and "gentlewoman" Hannah Owens (Peters) Jarvis (1763-1845) included a recipe for preserving eggs in her diary: *"Dip them in a very soft mixture of salt and clay – when dry cover with dry ashes and they will keep two years."*[24]

A Rough Start in Life

Hannah Peters Jarvis's riches-to-rags story began when she was born to wealthy parents in Connecticut. Her mother died when Hannah was just two. Her father, Reverend Samuel Peters, an Anglican minister, was declared a spy for including the names of the royal family in his prayers. He fled to England, leaving 11-year-old Hannah behind in the United States. Two years later Hannah joined her father.

In 1785, Hannah married fellow loyalist William Jarvis in England. Seven years later, the couple and their three children moved to Newark (later to be Niagara-on-the Lake), where, on the recommendation of Lieutenant Governor Simcoe, William Jarvis took up the position of provincial secretary and registrar of Upper Canada. Though they were part of the aristocracy of Upper Canada, behind the scenes things were going rather badly for the Jarvis family, whose numbers now included seven children.

Hannah Owen Jarvis (née Peters) with her daughters by James Earl (1791-1792)

They felt that there was a strong bias against American loyalists and on top of that, the Jarvis's excessive extravagance and out-of-control spending was taking a toll. To add to their woes, Hannah Jarvis detested Elizabeth Posthuma Simcoe, the wife of Governor Simcoe, to whom William Jarvis reported. Hannah called Elizabeth a "little stuttering Vixon," and resented Elizabeth's parsimony.

Thrust into Poverty

When William Jarvis died in 1817, he was bankrupt. Hannah Jarvis, who had once had servants and slaves and who had owned the first carriage in Upper Canada, was reduced to a life of poverty.

Hannah moved in with her daughter, Hannah Owen, whose husband, Alexander Hamilton, died in 1839, leaving his mother-in-law, his pregnant wife, and the couple's nine children penniless. Remarkably Hannah Jarvis was not deterred, rather she rallied and took in sewing to save the family from destitution, while also looking after her grandchildren, keeping the vegetable garden and tending to the poultry. By the time she died in 1845, despite all the difficulties, Hannah Jarvis had grown to love her life in Upper Canada.

* * *

Three recipes for preserving eggs were also included in *The Home Cook Book*, published in Toronto in 1877 for the benefit of the Hospital for Sick Children.

The hospital's treasurer, Mrs. Samuel McMaster wrote the book's preface. This version for preserving eggs was submitted by Mrs. McMaster's mother, Mrs. G. Wyllie.[25]

To Preserve Eggs

One pint salt, two pints fresh lime, three gallons water; mix well and put in eggs without cracking the shell; they must be kept covered with the brine.

Asparagus with Eggs

Addapted from newspaper clipping below

One bunch of asparagus
2 tbsp butter
Salt and pepper to taste
4 eggs, separated
2 tbsp milk or cream
1 (additional) tbsp. butter, warmed

Trim and boil a bunch of asparagus for 5-8 minutes or until just tender. While the asparagus is boiling, butter a deep pie dish, square glass pan, or equivalent. Set oven to 350°F.
Beat the 4 egg whites until stiff and set aside. In another bowl, beat the 4 egg yolks, milk or cream, and melted butter, and season lightly with salt and pepper. Mix the beaten egg whites into the egg yolk mixture. Drain the asparagus and lay the spears in the prepared baking dish. Pour egg mix evenly over the asparagus. Bake about 10-12 minutes at 350°F or until eggs are set.

SDAY, AUGUST 23, 1910.

RECIPES FROM
MARY'S COOK-BOOK

Asparagus With Eggs.

Boil a bunch of asparagus twenty minutes; cut off the tender tops and lay them in a deep pie plate, buttering, salting and peppering well. Beat up four eggs, the yolks and whites separately, to a stiff froth; add two tablespoonfuls of milk or cream, a tablespoonful of warm butter, pepper and salt to taste. Pour evenly over the asparagus mixture. Bake eight minutes or until the eggs are set.

Canada's EGG Opportunity

Britain's Shortage due to War
124,786,750 DOZ.

Britain Normally buys
190,850,520 DOZ.

2 Years ago Canada Sold
2,128,500 DOZ.

16 Years ago Canada Sold
10,860,536 DOZ.

"Very little eggs for such a big bird"
CANADA must do better.

(Top) Asparagus with Eggs from the *Ottawa Evening Journal*, Tuesday, August 23, 1910

(Right) Canada's Egg Opportunity circa 1918 - Canada Food Board Poster

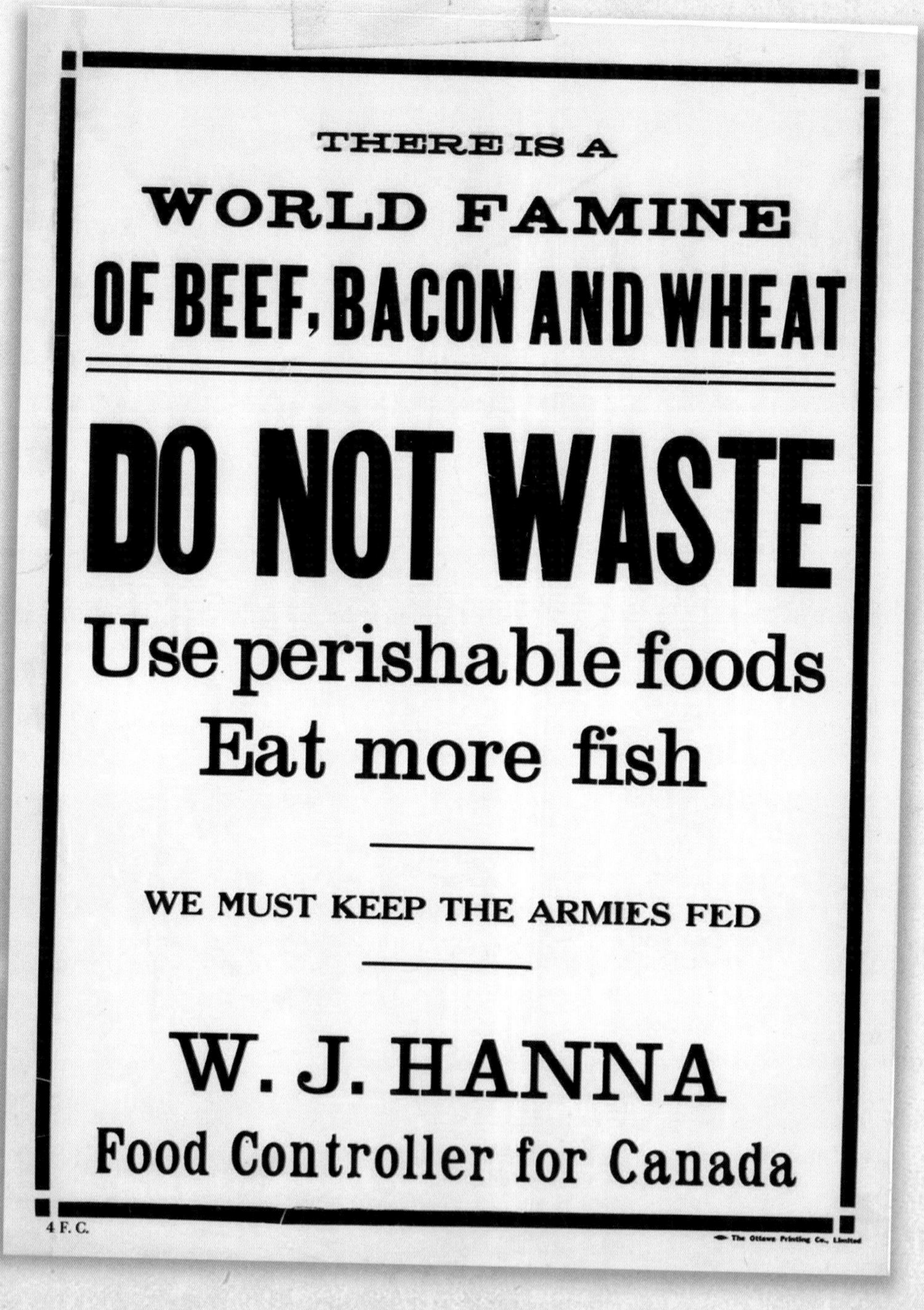

THERE IS A
WORLD FAMINE
OF BEEF, BACON AND WHEAT

DO NOT WASTE

Use perishable foods
Eat more fish

WE MUST KEEP THE ARMIES FED

W. J. HANNA
Food Controller for Canada

4 F. C.

The Ottawa Printing Co., Limited

NELLIE MCCLUNG – ONTARIO GIRL

"Never retreat, never explain, never apologize. Get the thing done and let them howl."
– Nellie McClung

The list of things that Nellie McClung has been called is astonishingly long: a first wave feminist, Canada's most famous suffragist, a lifelong women's rights activist, prolific author, social reformer, teacher, public lecturer, temperance movement advocate, member of the Canadian Broadcasting Corporation's first board of governors, a delegate to the League of Nations, Liberal Party Member of the Legislative Assembly (MLA) for Edmonton, and legislator. She was a wife, mother of five, and a grandmother. She was also, rather notably, a devoted cook.

Nellie McClung got things done.

But the thing that Nellie McClung is perhaps most noted for, is her role as one of the Famous Five: the group of five women who in 1927 petitioned the Supreme Court of Canada to have women officially declared as "persons."

On March 14, 1928, the Supreme Court ruled that women were not persons, as it related to Section 24 of the British North America Act.

Nellie McClung, 1914 by Cyril Jessop

Undaunted, the Famous Five took the matter to Privy Council of Great Britain. On October 18, 1929, The Lord Chancellor, Viscount Sankey, announced the conclusion of the Judicial Committee of the Privy Council of Great Britain, overturning the decision made by the Supreme Court of Canada. Sankey announced that yes, women were persons and further that: "The exclusion of women from all public offices is a relic of days more barbarous than ours."

A Legend is Born

Nellie Letitia (Mooney) McClung was born October 20, 1873, in Chatsworth, Ontario. She died September 01, 1951 in Victoria, BC. In between, she lived in Manitoba and Alberta. When she was seven, her family moved west, travelling in a covered wagon, arriving in the prairies just in time for one of the hardest winters ever on record. Later she wrote in her autobiography, *Clearing in the West*, about her childhood memories of her family's journey from Ontario to Manitoba in 1880:

> *The log house had a thatched roof, made from prairie hay and was not chinked, but it had a floor of rough lumber… and one window facing west. One window might be thought insufficient for a house that must lodge eight people, but light and air came in unbidden through many openings; indeed, how to keep out the cold became our great problem. We brought a real stove with us and pipes and the first day saw it set in place and mother could then begin her bread, real bread, made with a Royal yeast cake, to displace the soda bannock, cooked in bacon grease, which had been the backbone of our diet on the journey.*

Early Food Writer

Nellie McClung often wrote about food. When she lost her seat as the MLA for Edmonton, she consoled herself in the kitchen. "I was seized with a desire to cook," she wrote in the second volume of her autobiography, *The Stream Runs Fast* , "I set off at once on a perfect debauch of cooking. I grated cheese, stoned dates, whipped cream and made salad dressing and I let the phone ring…. I got more comfort that day out of my cooking spree than I did from either my philosophy or my religion."[26]

(Below) This recipe for dumplings is from a recipe Nellie herself submitted to a small booklet called, *Cook To Win*, put out by the Good Cheer Club of Wesley United Church in Calgary, in 1943.

[Nellie McClung's] Dumplings

2 cups flour
4 tsp baking powder
1 tsp salt
4 tbsp shortening (lard or butter)
2/3 cup whole milk

Mix the flour, baking powder, and salt in a large bowl. Cut in the shortening until the mixture resembles coarse breadcrumbs. Add milk and mix to blend. Form into balls about 2 inches in diameter and drop into a pot of cooked, simmering chicken or beef stew. Cover pot and cook the stew and dumplings for another 15 minutes.

Cottolene shortening advertisement circa 1868

ANNA BROWNELL JAMESON RAMBLES & EATS THROUGH UPPER CANADA

Irish-born English writer and early feminist Anna Brownell (Murphy) Jameson (1794 – 1860) came to Canada in 1836 at the behest of her husband, Robert Sympson Jameson, the Attorney General of Upper Canada, from whom she was separated. When her husband failed to meet her in New York, she found her own way, in winter, to a cold, snowy and unwelcoming Toronto. She lasted just less than a year in Canada during which time she began making notes for *Winter Studies and Summer Rambles in Canada*, published in Britain in 1838.

Anna Brownell Jameson, artist and date unknown

A little Ill-built Town

Jameson was torn about Canada. She described Toronto as, "most strangely mean and melancholy. A little ill-built town…" but given that she arrived alone, in winter, perhaps this was more a reflection of her feelings about the state of her marriage, which though an intellectual match, seemed a failure on most other fronts.

She was much happier the following summer, exploring Lake Huron from within a canoe, and seemed particularly enamoured of the Indigenous steersman, Martin… "who, in a cotton shirt, arms bared to the shoulder, loose trousers, a scarlet sash round his waist, richly embroidered with beads, and his long black hair waving, took his place in the stern … The manner in which he stood, turning and twisting himself with the agility of a snake, and striking first on one side, then on the other, was graceful and picturesque."[27]

Canoe on Lake Huron, by Anna Brownell Jameson, 1837

On her canoe trip, Jameson dined on broiled and fried trout, bass, and pigeons, ate quantities of gooseberries and wild raspberries, and drank "good madeira." She slept in tents on beds of boughs topped with bearskins and blankets. The canoe trip lasted nine nights, and when it ended she pined "for nights passed in the open air or on rocks, or boards."

Brown Trout

Later she wrote about one night when they had been camped on a rock ledge at the edge of the lake; "I wish I could give you the least idea of the beauty of this evening; but when I try to put in words what was before me, the sense of its ineffable loveliness overpowers me now, even as it did then."[28]

A Dash of Salt
Of the food during her stay in Toronto she reported, "Quantities of salted provisions are still imported into the country for the consumption of the soldiers and the distant settlers, and at certain seasons – at present, for example – there is some difficulty in procuring anything else."

Her table, she admitted, if somewhat begrudgingly, was pretty well supplied.

"Beef is tolerable but lean;" she wrote, "Mutton bad, scarce, and dearer than beef; pork excellent and delicate, being fattened principally on Indian corn. The fish is of many various kinds, and delicious. During the whole winter we had black-bass and white-fish, caught in holes in the ice, and brought down by the Indians. Venison, game, and wild fowl are always to be had; the quails, which are caught in immense numbers near Toronto, are most delicate eating. I lived on them when I could eat nothing else. What they call partridge here is a small species of pheasant, also very good; and now we are promised snipes and woodcocks in abundance. The wild goose is also excellent eating when well cooked…."[29]

THE EVOLUTION OF IRISH STEW

Sheep thrived in Ireland where they were more suited than cattle to the small farms of Irish tenant farmers. Hardy and tenacious animals, sheep were also versatile – being useful and profitable for their wool, milk (much of which was used in cheese production), and finally, once they had reached the end of their productive years, they were used for their meat. As a result, mutton was much more commonly available and much less expensive than lamb.

Since mutton tends to be both slightly tough, and stronger in flavour, it lends itself perfectly to slow cooking and hence its association with stew. A traditional Irish stew was originally made from very few ingredients: mutton, onions, potatoes, and seasonings.

Hurrah for an Irish stew

Hurrah for an Irish stew,
It's season'd so fine, and its flavour's divine,
Hurrah for an Irish stew.
It's good with pepper and salt,
It's good with potatoes a few,
There's nought can equal, in this grubbing world,
An elegant Irish stew.

If you'd ask a young lover to dine,
And have him prove kind unto you,
To make love come out of his beautiful mouth,
You should stuff it with Irish stew.
Then hurrah for an Irish stew,
Hurrah for an Irish stew,
It's season'd so fine, and its flavour's divine,
Hurrah for an Irish stew.[30]

The ballad, "Hurrah for an Irish Stew," by J. Bruce Wright , contained the recipe for Irish Stew within its lines:

When large numbers of Irish immigrants began arriving in the New World in the 1800s, their traditional recipes such as mutton stew began to evolve to include local ingredients, such as beef in place of mutton and a wider variety of vegetables and seasonings. Eventually, stock and later Guinness or other stout beers were also added to the stew in place of water – helping to tenderize tougher cuts of meat and also add flavour.

Classic Irish Stew
This recipe, a slightly adapted version of an old Irish stew recipe, was handed down to a friend, and then passed along to me. It has become a family favourite. Serve with buttered, mashed turnip and either dumplings or Irish soda bread.

Vintage sheep illustration showing cuts of mutton.

Classic Irish Stew

3 tbsp olive oil
2-3 lbs (1- 1.4 kg) stew beef, cut in pieces
2 onions, diced
2 cloves garlic, minced
4 medium potatoes, peeled, and quartered
2 tbsp all purpose flour
1 440 ml can of Guinness or other dark stout beer
½ cup beef stock
2 tsp dried thyme
2 bay leaves
1 tsp salt
½ tsp ground black pepper

In a large (oven-proof) stew pot, over medium-high, warm the oil and briefly sauté the onion and the garlic (about two minutes). Add the beef and continue to sauté until the vegetables and beef are gently browned. Stir in the flour, distributing evenly throughout. Pour in the beer and stock. Stir in the thyme, salt and pepper and add the bay leaves. Turn heat down (low should suffice) and cover. Simmer on stovetop on low, or cook in the oven at 275°F, for 2 ½ to 3 hours. Check intermittently to make sure there is enough liquid. If not, add water, ½ cup at a time. Before serving, remove bay leaves and thicken stew with a flour water slurry, if necessary.

HOW TO COOK A DEER

Photograph of Nettie Jane Wallace Leonard and others in front of farmhouse, 1908

Nettie Jane (Wallace) Leonard, (1884-1982) was born, raised, and lived in Hartington, Ontario for all but the last 10 years of her very long life, when she lived with family in Napanee. Nettie Jane is pictured below (fourth from the left, front row, dressed in white) in front of the family farmhouse. When this photograph was taken in 1908, she was 24 years old and a new bride.

The women in the photograph were gathered together to prepare food for the hired hands who came seasonally to the farm to get the crops into the ground, and then later returned for the harvest. Threshing (harvesting grain and removing the seeds from the stalks or husks) was an incredibly laborious job, accounting for about one quarter of all agricultural labour before threshing machines became commonplace.

Threshing or thrashing (it was known both ways) was hard, hungry work and Nettie Jane never forgot peeling the mountains of potatoes needed to feed the men for their noontime dinner, every day during threshing season.

Nettie Jane was both incredibly good-natured and a famously good cook. In her recipe collection are many treasures, written in her distinctive handwriting. She was known for, among other things, her white layer cake filled with lemon curd and her cookies.

This recipe, which might have been entitled "How to Cook Venison," is instead entitled, in completely straightforward fashion, "How to cook Deer." Not wanting to waste paper, she included a caramelized pudding sauce recipe on the same, well-used page.

Venison and other game meats were important to both Indigenous Peoples and settlers. Early settlers left the hunting to Indigenous people, who were far superior hunters, and instead exchanged goods such as salt pork and flour for venison, rabbit, moose, partridge, ducks, and other wild birds.

Any good cook of the era knew how to treat game meat and dress it with either gravy or sauces made from cranberries, blackberries, red currants, or dried currants reconstituted in a little port wine. Venison is very lean so benefits from being cooked in a little extra fat – bacon, butter, an olive oil marinade, or leftover pork or beef drippings, etc.

How to Cook Deer
Have water boiling put
in a handful of Salt
Let it boil 1/2 hour, then
put in the oven and
roast untill tender.

Sauce for Pudding
Burn 1 cup of Sugar & a
little water
Then 1 teaspoon Cornstarch
mixed with water
and small piece of
butter

LADY EATON'S STEWED LEG OF MUTTON

Flora McCrea was born in 1880, in Omemee, Ontario, a small community in the Kawartha Lakes. Flora, the youngest of eight children, was by all accounts a happy and hardworking child who left high school in her final year to look after her unwell older sister. That might have had a role in Flora's decision, at age 18, to move to Toronto and train as a nurse.

While at Rotherham House, a small private hospital in Toronto, Flora encountered a patient named John Craig Eaton, son of the founder and president of the T. Eaton Company. The two had many shared interests, including baseball, and soon found themselves in love. They married in 1901, and in 1909, in order to accommodate their growing family, they built Ardwold, a 50-room home, the biggest mansion Toronto had ever seen.

Ardwold, home of Sir John Eaton and Lady Eaton, Spadina Road, Toronto, circa 1910

When the First World War broke out, John and Flora Eaton implemented a number of measures to help Eaton's employees affected by the war. They offered full pay to any married male employee, and half pay to any single male employee of Eaton's, who volunteered to serve the war effort. The Eatons also volunteered to return any profits made by war contracts to the government and they used their home, Ardwold, to entertain soldiers and fundraise for war efforts.

In 1915, John Craig Eaton was knighted for his contributions to the war effort and Flora Eaton became Lady Eaton.

In 1922, 45-year-old Sir John Eaton died from pneumonia, leaving Lady Eaton an heiress and sole parent to their six children. Lady Eaton was also named as a Director of the T. Eaton Company. When she took up her position on the Board, she said, "I will accept the position on one condition:

that I shall always be treated as just another person on the Board and not as a woman." From then on, Lady Eaton became focused on company-employee relations and improvement of employee welfare and benefits. She served on the Board for 21 years.

Lady Eaton loved to travel and entertain and was a food aficionada, with a strong interest in what was then called "domestic science." She is credited with having brought Red Velvet Cake to Canada, which for many years was made by Eaton's Bakeries and served in the store restaurants like the elegant Georgian Room in Toronto.

The Wimodausis Club Cook Book

Lady Eaton submitted two recipes to the second edition of the *The Wimodausis Club Cook Book*, published in 1922 in Toronto. The Wimodausis Club was a Toronto women's volunteer social services group that took its name from the first syllables of the words: wives, mothers, daughters, sisters.

The following is Flora Eaton's recipe for Stewed Leg of Mutton. Since a leg of mutton is somewhat harder to come by these days, a leg of lamb is easily substituted. A "handful" of salt in the haricot beans may be a little more than necessary – a teaspoon would seem ample.

STEWED LEG OF MUTTON
Lady Eaton.

Melt three tablespoonfuls of good dripping in the stewpan and in it fry the leg of mutton, turning it frequently till it is nicely colored all over. Add one pint of water, pepper, salt, two laurel leaves and a sprig of thyme. Under the leg of mutton in the pan lay a big slice of fat bacon or fat salt pork. Cover the pan and stew gently but not too slowly for five hours. At the same time boil a good pan of haricot beans in plain water; salt in the water turns haricot beans hard. Strain your beans. Add a good handful of salt and toss them thoroughly in it. Make a bed of them on a big dish and pour all the mutton gravy over it. Then slice the mutton thinly and arrange it on top. You can make a bed of mashed potatoes if you like, but the haricots are more really French. They must be boiled till they are all broken and coming out of their skins.

Mint Sauce

Pick mint leaves off the stalks; wash and dry them carefully; chop them with a sharp knife very quickly, to preserve their green color; put it into a boat [i.e., sauce boat]; add sufficient vinegar to make it liquid, and powdered sugar to take off the acidity of the vinegar.

Mint Sauce for Roast Lamb from *The Canadian Housewife's Manual of Cookery*, 1861

PRESERVING FOOD AND SALTING AND SMOKING MEAT

The preservation of food before the advent of refrigeration was no small task. By late summer and well into the autumn each year, a huge amount of time and effort was dedicated to putting down food, as well as firewood or coal, for the coming winter months.

Everything possible was either jellied, pickled, smoked, salted, dried, or buried. A note in the *Cornwall Freeholder* on December 13, 1867, advised how to keep vegetables during the cold winter months, ***"...in a cellar covered in earth and sand or in a well-drained pit with alternate layers of roots and sand covered over with earth."***

Mushrooms, peas, beans, strawberries, cherries, apples, quinces, squash and pumpkin were dried. Currants, blueberries, chokecherries, grapes, gooseberries, and plums were made into jams, jellies, or wine. Cucumber, cabbage, cauliflower, pears, walnuts, eggs, and apples were pickled or preserved in brine. Potatoes, turnips, and cabbages were buried in the ground. Onions, carrots, and beets were stored in sawdust in wooden bins. Chestnuts, butternuts, and hickory nuts were dried in the sun. Sage, rosemary, and thyme were hung in bunches. Honey and maple syrup were stored in jars or crocks. Fish were dried and salted. Beef was salted or smoked. Pigs were butchered, and ham and bacon were pickled or smoked. Sausage meat was stuffed into casings and packed in stone crocks, sealed with lard. It was salt pork though, that was the mainstay – a dish that quickly grew monotonous to the palate but was absolutely imperative for survival.

Surviving Wholly on Salt at HBC'S Fort Moose

Moose Factory, on a tiny island in the Moose River, near the southern end of James Bay, in northern Ontario, was the first English-speaking settlement in Upper Canada. It was also the site of the second Hudson's Bay Company (HBC) trading post, Fort Moose, built in 1673. Fort Moose was captured by the French in 1686 and returned to the Hudson's Bay Company in 1713. Moose Factory takes its name from the proliferation of moose and the term "factor", which was the jurisdiction of the Hudson's Bay Company merchant in charge of buying and selling.

SALTING PORK.

A. M. G.

Cover the bottom of the barrel with salt an inch deep; put down one layer of pork and cover that with salt half an inch thick; continue this until all your pork is disposed of; then cover the whole with strong brine; pack as tight as possible, the rind side down or next to the barrel; keep the pork always under the brine by using an inner cover and clean stones. Should any scum arise, pour off the brine, scald it, and add more salt. Old brine can be boiled down, well skimmed, and used for a fresh supply.

A GOOD MODE OF SMOKING MEAT.

Mrs. Thomas McKay.

Get a sugar hogshead, knock out the bottom, and set over a smoking fire of corn-cobs, walnut, maple or hickory, and a considerable share of dried dung. Cover it with boards.

(Top) How to Salt Pork from *The Home Cook Book*, 1877

(Above) Beef was often smoked for use over winter. This method, from *The Canadian Economist*, 1881, calls for a sugar hogshead – a very large barrel used to hold sugar; as well as a "considerable share of dried dung."

Life on the remote trading posts was incredibly difficult. There were all the regular aspects of life to contend with – food, shelter, clothing, laundry and sanitation, plus of course the care of the ill, religious ministrations, defence, education, and entertainment. And then there was all the paperwork and accounting – it was a business operation after all.

In 1783, Moose Fort had a chief, a second in command, a surgeon, two clerks, a carpenter, a cooper, a bricklayer, two tailors, an armourer, 15 labourers, and a number of others connected to the ships that brought people and goods in and out, when the weather allowed.[31]

Food was a major challenge for the staff at Moose Fort. Liquor, wine, beer, beef, pork, oatmeal, flour and other basics were brought in but required much advance planning and supplies could not always be counted upon. Vegetables and fruit were scarce. Bread was made on site. Fish and game comprised the major part of the diet. Salted food was imperative in order to survive the long, harsh winters.

The chief recorded the following in his journal in January 1785, "I had a tolerable Goose hunt having salted 20 casks and I have received a few rabbits from Indians during the winter, with which, and the Beef and Pork we have been pretty well off for fresh food till Christmas since which we have lived almost wholly on salt."[32]

A SLICE OF HUMBLE PIE

Before January 1858, when Queen Victoria chose Ottawa as the capital of the emerging nation of Canada, other cities including Kingston and Montreal had briefly held the honour. For a short time, to appease both the English and French factions, the capital actually alternated between Quebec City and Toronto – necessitating the moving of not just the members of parliament and their families and households, but also all the employees, all manner of equipment and furniture, and a huge volume of government files and equipment, every four years.

'Let us be Canadians'

John A. Macdonald, who had been a member of parliament during the years leading up to the decision about the new capital, was a passionate advocate for a Canada that included both English and French interests. "Let us be English or let us be French," he once famously stated, "but above all let us be Canadians."

Macdonald believed the similarities between the two cultures outweighed the differences and he also believed that French and English-speaking Canadians had more in common with each other than they did with Americans. The French and English might have been separated by language but they were united by similarities in their European culture.

Perhaps nowhere were the similarities between the two more obvious than in their culinary preferences. Meat pie for example, was a favourite of both cultures. Tourtière, the legendary French-Canadian meat pie, was remarkably similar to an old-fashioned Yorkshire pork pie whose ingredients are typically finely chopped pork, water, salt, pepper, and powdered sage.

Other British meat pies including Scotch pie (typically filled with minced lamb or mutton), or the Melton Mowbray (raised) pie, which was filled with chopped or ground pork and an aspic mixture, were also similar to the beloved tourtière. Macdonald and his English-speaking colleagues would have been right at home in the gas-lit taverns of Montreal, eating tourtière washed down with claret or ale.

Les Tourtes

The name tourtière is thought to have derived from either a cooking vessel of the same name or perhaps from the fact that early tourtières were made using passenger pigeons, known in French as les tourtes.

Meat pies were once the domain of the wealthy in medieval Europe. Before metal or glass baking dishes became commonplace, thick pastry was used to encase a meat filling – acting as both a cooking container and a way of preserving the meat, at least temporarily. The pastry was often used to thicken soups fed to servants and the less fortunate.

Pies made from leftover scraps and less desirable bits of meat, (heart, liver, lungs and kidneys) were referred to as "umble" perhaps stemming from the word humble, or possibly from the French "nomble," (deer's innards). The pies fed to servants gave rise to the expression "eating humble pie."

Tourtière

Pastry for a double crust pie
1 ½ pounds pork
1 onion, very finely diced
1 tbsp flour
1 tsp salt
¼ tsp pepper
1 tsp dried sage
½ cup water

Roll out the pastry and line a 9-inch pie plate.
Fry the pork and onion together over medium low heat for about 12 minutes, or until meat is no longer pink. Drain off most of the fat and reserve separately for other uses – a little can remain behind for flavouring.

Set oven to 400°F.

Add the flour, salt, pepper and sage to the meat mixture and stir to distribute. Add water and bring to the boil, turn heat down and cook a minute or two longer until the mixture is slightly thickened. It should be quite a damp mixture, not dry. If it is too dry – add another couple of tablespoons of water and another tablespoon of the pork fat.

Spoon mixture into pastry-lined pie plate. Damp around the edge of the pastry with a wet pastry brush. Roll out the top pastry and seal the pie using the tines of a fork to press around the edge. Use any leftover pastry to decorate the top with leaves, or make a small pig using a cookie cutter. Pierce the pastry in several places.

Bake at 400°F for about 35 minutes. Check at 25 and if the top is browning too quickly, turn heat back to 325 and continue baking another 5-10 minutes.

CHICKEN PIES GALORE

Chicken pies of one kind or another have been cropping up in cookbooks for a very long time. Hannah Glasse published a recipe for Chicken Pye in her 1747 book, *The Art of Cookery*.

Glasse also included a recipe for a Yorkshire Christmas Pye, which called for a large, boned turkey, a goose, a fowl, a partridge, a pigeon, an unspecified number of woodcocks, more game and "what sort of wild fowl you can get." All of this, plus stuffing, was laid in a substantial crust, topped with "at least four pounds of butter," and finished with another layer of pastry, then baked in a very hot oven for four hours or more. "This crust," she wrote, "will take a bushel of flour."

Yorkshire Christmas pyes, Glasse noted, were often sent to London as presents. An article in the *Newcastle Chronicle* in January 1770 reported on a pie with a nine-foot circumference, weighing at least 12 stone (168 pounds), which had been shipped to London in a special pie case fitted with four wheels.

Chicken Pie
By comparison to the Yorkshire Christmas Pye, this chicken pie from *The Cook Not Mad* looks positively simple.

No 49.   Chicken Pie.

Take two chickens, joint and put them in a pot with four ounces of pork cut in slices, add pepper and salt, boil until tender, turn them out and set away to cool; make a rich paste, with which line the dish half an inch thick, then a layer of chicken with pieces of butter, and sprinkle on pepper and flour; put on your gravy from the chickens, and continue to do so until filled up; roll out a thick crust, bake an hour in a hot oven; serve it up with melted butter and any seasoning you like.

Chicken Pot Pie and the Arcadian Court Restaurant
When the Arcadian Court restaurant in Toronto's Yonge Street Simpson's department store opened on March 11, 1929, at the very beginning of the Great Depression, it was an immediate hit. Canada had never seen anything like it. With its 40-foot ceilings, massive Art Deco chandeliers, grand arches, and seating for a thousand, it was the largest dining room in the country.

Beloved by many

The Arcadian Court quickly became a beloved institution, famous for its signature dish, chicken pot pie. Soon after, various versions of chicken pot pie recipes began appearing in cookbooks and magazines across Canada.

Chicken Pot Pie

1 small cooked chicken, deboned and chopped
1 heaping tablespoon butter
1 heaping tablespoon flour
2 cups (500ml) chicken stock or milk or a mixture of both
½ tsp salt
¼ tsp pepper
[1-2 cups cooked vegetables as desired including sautéed diced onion and mushrooms, steamed peas, cooked diced carrots and peeled, chopped cooked potatoes]
Biscuit Topping
1 cup flour
2 tsp Watkins [or any other] baking powder
½ tsp salt
2 level tablespoons of lard [or butter]
½ cup (125ml) milk

For the pie:
Butter a large deep pie dish or equivalent. Set aside. Melt the butter in a saucepan and add the flour. Add the chicken stock or milk and stir well. Add salt and pepper and cook until thickened. Add the chicken and vegetables. Leave on low heat to stay warm while you prepare the topping.

For the topping:
Sift together the flour, baking powder, and salt. Cut in the shortening until mixture resembles fine crumbs. Add the milk to make a soft dough. If the mix is too dry, add another tablespoon or two of milk. Do not overmix. Turn onto a lightly floured board and knead gently 3 or 4 times. Roll out to make a topping the approximate size of the prepared baking dish. Spoon the warm filling into the prepared pie dish. Place the biscuit topping on top of the chicken mixture. Bake at 375°F (190°C) for about 25 minutes or until biscuit top is golden brown and cooked through.

WATKINS COOK BOOK

CHICKEN PIE

(Top) Chicken Pot Pie, adapted from the *Watkins Cook Book*, 1925

(Right) Chicken pot pie illustration from *Watkins Cook Book*

MRS. BEETON'S BESTSELLER

When *Mrs. Beeton's Book of Household Management* was published by her husband, Samuel Beeton, in 1861, nobody could have foreseen the extraordinary and lasting success the book would become. Isabella Mary Beeton (1836–1865) was just 20 years old when she married publisher and magazine editor Samuel Beeton in 1856. A year later she was writing a food column for *The Englishwoman's Domestic Magazine*, one of her husband's publications.

Mrs. Beeton was not much of a cook and was accused of copying and plagiarizing many of her recipes for both her food column and later in her book. Despite this, her book sold more than sixty thousand copies in its first year and nearly two million copies by 1868. Even by today's standards those numbers are impressive.

A Life Cut Short

Isabella Beeton died of fever in 1865, at the age of 28, cutting short a rather tragic life. She gave birth to four children, only two of whom lived past infancy, and she also had several miscarriages. It was suspected that Samuel Beeton had contracted syphilis through encounters with prostitutes and had unknowingly infected Isabella.

Down on his luck, Samuel Beeton sold the rights to *The Book of Household Management*. The new publishing company, Ward Lock and Tyler, suppressed the information about the death of Isabella and continued publishing her book as though she were still alive.

Mrs. Beeton's Book of Household Management has been in continuous print since 1861 and remains one of the most successful cookbooks of all time, and a definitive source of information about food and culinary history in the 19th and 20th centuries. Many copies found their way to Canada and are still in use today.

VEAL AND HAM PIE.   From *Mrs. Beeton's Book of Household Management*

898. INGREDIENTS.—2 lbs. of veal cutlets, 1/2 lb. of boiled ham, 2 tablespoonfuls of minced savoury herbs, 1/4 teaspoonful of grated nutmeg, 2 blades of pounded mace, pepper and salt to taste, a strip of lemon-peel finely minced, the yolks of 2 hard-boiled eggs, 1/2 pint of water, nearly 1/2 pint of good strong gravy, puff-crust.

Mode.—Cut the veal into nice square pieces, and put a layer of them at the bottom of a pie-dish; sprinkle over these a portion of the herbs, spices, seasoning, lemon-peel, and the yolks of the eggs cut in slices; cut the ham very thin, and put a layer of this in. Proceed in this manner until the dish is full, so arranging it that the ham comes at the top. Lay a puff-paste on the edge of the dish, and pour in about 1/2 pint of water; cover with crust, ornament it with leaves, brush it over with the yolk of an egg, and bake in a well-heated oven for 1 to 1-1/2 hour, or longer, should the pie be very large.

When it is taken out of the oven, pour in at the top, through a funnel, nearly 1/2 pint of strong gravy: this should be made sufficiently good that, when cold, it may cut in a firm jelly. This pie may be very much enriched by adding a few mushrooms, oysters, or sweet-breads; but it will be found very good without any of the last-named additions. Time.—1-1/2 hour, or longer, should the pie be very large. Average cost, 3s. Sufficient for 5 or 6 persons. Seasonable from March to October.

LADY MACDONALD MAKES PASTRY

Lady Susan Agnes (Bernard) Macdonald (1836-1920), second wife of Sir John A. Macdonald, was a Jamaican-born Englishwoman, 21 years younger than John A. She didn't come naturally to cooking, though she certainly understood the importance of food and hospitality.

Raised Pie [Pastry]

The crust for Raised Pies is made With ½ Lb. Butter to Every pound of Flour, to be mixed with hot Water and left to Get a little Cold before it is put into the Shape [Springform pan.]. Shape must be one which can be taken to pieces.

This recipe for pastry comes from Lady Agnes Macdonald's manuscript receipt book.

Lady Susan Agnes Macdonald by William James Topley, Ottawa, May 1868

TALKING TURKEY

Turkeys are native to North America, where the flightless birds were first domesticated around 800 BCE by the Indigenous Peoples of Mexico. Cortés, the Spanish Conquistador, is thought to have been the first to bring turkeys back to Spain, around 1519. Soon the birds were found throughout Europe and by 1541 they were in England, where for various reasons, including the fact that the Turkish Ottoman Empire was at its peak, the large rather exotic birds came by their current name.

General Stovin's Turkeys

In Canada, in 1814, General Stovin (1783 –1865) a British Army officer who served throughout the War of 1812, wasn't happy and was taking it out on the troops and ordering them, even those on leave, to report to duty at six in the morning, daily. Turns out the General, who was also a gourmand, had been raising turkeys, keeping them in separate pens, and feeding them different diets, to see how they fared and which produced better tasting, more succulent meat.

Stovin must have been looking forward to a great feast where the birds were sampled and savoured and the merits of each discussed. But the underlings got wind of the General's plan and even though there was a sentry keeping watch, "… some military foxes scaled the fences and captured the Turkies, making a confidential report to Him [Gen. Stovin] on the barlied [barley-ed], wheated, or riced meats."[33]

Roast Turkey

Have a turkey well picked, washed, and thoroughly dried. Prepare a stuffing... [see chestnut stuffing below or use other preferred stuffing]. Fill the breast and body with the stuffing, sew up the opening, truss it and put it in a pan to roast. Baste often. When done make a brown gravy...

Chestnut Stuffing

2 cups chestnuts
½ cup melted fat [butter]
1 cup cracker [or dry bread] crumbs
¾ teaspoon salt
Few grains pepper
¾ cup cream

Blanch and shell chestnuts. Cook in boiling salted water until soft. Drain and mash. Add half the butter, salt, pepper, and cream. Melt remaining fat, mix with cracker crumbs, then combine mixtures.

Apple Stuffing

Take half a pound of the pulp of tart apples which have been baked or scalded; add two ounces of breadcrumbs, some powdered sage, and a finely shred onion; season with cayenne pepper.

(Above Left) Roast Turkey from *Dora's Cook Book* 1888

(Above Right) Chestnut Stuffing from *The Metropolitan Life Cook Book*, 1918

(Left) Apple Stuffing from *Dora's Cook Book* 1888

THE (NEARLY) UBIQUITOUS CABBAGE ROLL

Cabbage rolls are Polish. They're Russian, German, Finnish, Swedish. And also Icelandic, Japanese, Mennonite, and Jewish. Cabbage rolls are eaten in Azerbaijan, Argentina, Ukraine, Romania, Moldova, Greece, Hungary, Bosnia and Herzegovina, Macedonia, Bulgaria, Croatia, and Serbia. In Egypt, Sudan, Korea, Israel, Albania, Turkey, Lithuania, Estonia. The list goes on: South America, North America, China, Iran, Vietnam.

In Quebec, cabbage rolls go by the quaint name, cigares au chou. In Ukraine they're holubtsi, meaning little pigeons. In Argentina, the Dominican Republic, Ecuador, Mexico, and Chile they're known as niños envueltos – wrapped-up children; and in Germany and Austria: krautwickel.

Cabbage rolls have been part of the Jewish culinary repertoire for at least two thousand years.

The humble cabbage roll is nearly universal, though curiously it is not present in British or Irish cuisine, despite the popularity of cabbage, especially in Irish cooking.

(Above) Margaret Lang, right, at the community baseball diamond in Trout Creek, Ontario, circa 1945

Came with the Mennonites

Here in Ontario, cabbage rolls have been on the menu since the first wave of Mennonites arrived in 1786. The rolls are typically made with either ground pork or beef, or a blend of the two, mixed with rice, onions and seasonings, and served in a tomato sauce.

This recipe comes from, Margaret (Lang) Mechefske (1927-2005), an extraordinarily talented cook who regularly won all the blue ribbons for baking, breadmaking, and preserving at her local Northern Ontario fall fair. Marg was a beacon of kindness who could always be counted on to take the high road.

She spent her whole life on a farm. She milked cows, gathered eggs, managed the finances, maintained a massive vegetable garden, quilted, was active in the community, drove children to hockey and other events, cleaned house, wiped noses, spanked bottoms when necessary (it was a different era), and still had time to turn out a delicious dinner, night after night after night. She learned to make these cabbage rolls from her mother, Rachel (Hummel) Lang.

Cabbage Rolls

I large head of cabbage, large tough outer leaves removed
(feed to the pigs!)
I ½ pounds (680 grams) ground beef (can mix with ground
pork if desired)
¾ cup uncooked, long grain rice
I large onion, finely diced
I egg
I tsp salt, good grinding of pepper,
I clove garlic, minced
Sauce:
2 cans tomato soup
2 cans water
2 tbsp sugar

Boil the cabbage whole for 5-7 minutes. Let cool before
separating the leaves. You will need about 12 good-sized
leaves. Where necessary, make a V-shaped cut to remove
the coarse parts of the spine from the bottoms of
the leaves.

Mix the (raw) meat, uncooked rice, onion, egg, salt, pepper,
and minced garlic.

Lay the leaves out and divide the meat mixture evenly
between them. Wrap as tightly as possible, tucking the end
bits in with your fingers as best possible.

Lay the rolls into a large Dutch oven or shallow roast pan
with a lid.

Mix the sauce ingredients together in a saucepan and bring
to a boil. Pour over the rolls.

Bake covered at 350°F for I ½ hours, then uncovered for
an hour, adding a little water if the rolls start to look dry.

THE NEW FOOD CONTROLLER DOES SOME MANSPLAINING

War has always had a big impact on food and food security. Food, in times of war, becomes both a weapon and an instrument of power.

During the First World War, with hundreds of thousands of Canadians away serving the war effort, farming and food distribution were severely impacted. All those left at home still required food. At the same time, troops required rations. And to complicate matters, merchant ships carrying supplies were being specifically targeted by German U-boats, resulting in heavy losses of food shipments. A shortage of food drove prices upwards and this encouraged hoarding, creating a dangerous, vicious cycle.

'Farmerettes'

In Ontario, the government introduced the Farm Services Corps, or "Farmerettes," a program aimed primarily at women, who were recruited to do a wide variety of farm work that might otherwise have been done by men who were off fighting in the war.

On the home front, the Canadian Government was determined to focus on food-control measures such as "national self denial" and voluntary conservation, preservation, and ingredient substitution, rather than enforced rationing. The public were asked not to waste or hoard food, and to limit their consumption of scarce commodities including beef, bacon, wheat, sugar, eggs, and butter. Canadians were told to waste less and to preserve food for the winter. Most of the requests were aimed at women.

On June 21, 1917, William J. Hanna was appointed Canada's new Food Controller. The position was controversial and on January 24, 1918, six months after he had taken the role on, Hanna resigned. But in the meantime, he introduced a number of measures including a series of war menus published in newspapers throughout the country, as well as posters, booklets, and food pledge service cards for households to place in visible locations as part of their patriotic duty.

A July 1917 letter addressed, "To the Women of Canada," implored, "The rigid conservation of food materials and the most complete elimination of household waste are objects of supreme national importance during this world crisis… Surely no Canadian woman, however affluent can lightly dismiss responsibilities of so grave a nature. [Signed] W. J. Hanna, Food Controller."

CANADA

TO WIN THE WAR
THIS HOUSEHOLD
IS PLEDGED
TO CARRY OUT CONSCIENTIOUSLY
THE ADVICE AND DIRECTIONS
OF THE
FOOD CONTROLLER

Hanna's letter came from a booklet entitled, How to Live in Wartime, which also included menu ideas and nutritional advice. For breakfast he suggested fruits, oatmeal or various prepared cereals, and toast, or other similar options, including eggs, baked beans, and coffee tea, cocoa, milk or water. The lunch and dinner menus were similarly predictable, though they reminded readers of the need to save beef and bacon. In place of beef, for example, the booklet suggested, "Use other meats instead…" The instructions continued, as though most Canadian women might be quite new to the kitchen.

With or without Food Controller Hanna at the helm, women were already scrimping and saving, gardening, foraging, pickling, preserving, and feeding families on whatever they could find and cook.

Soaring inflation and shortages had already seen to that. This recipe, for Vegetable Toad-in-the-Hole, from *The Family Herald Cook Book*, was representative of a new way of cooking, using much less meat.

VEGETABLE TOAD-IN-THE-HOLE

One cup of beans, peas, or lentils cooked; one cup of cooked root vegetables. These may be mixed in any proportion. Season nicely with parsley, salt, pepper and herbs. Spread in a buttered baking dish. Cover with bits of dripping and an ounce of grated cheese. Have ready a pancake batter made with one egg and let it stand at least an hour. Add the baking powder just before using. Pour this batter over the vegetables and bake slowly until risen. Serve when brown.

Bits of bacon, cold meat or sausages may be added to the vegetables and require a little longer cooking.

One Egg Pancake Batter

1 cup flour
2 ½ tsp baking powder
½ tsp salt
1 cup milk
2 tbsp melted butter
1 egg, beaten

In a mixing bowl, stir together the flour, baking powder, and salt. Make a well in the centre and add the milk, melted butter, and beaten egg. Pour over the Vegetable Toad-in-the-Hole and cook as per the instructions above.

Patriotic Canadians Will Not Hoard Food - WWI Food Poster, circa 1918

WINNIE COLLVER'S SUPPER DISH

Allie Winnifred (Nelles) Collver, 1911-2002, was always known as Winnie. She was born and raised in Bealton, Ontario, and lived her entire life in Norfolk County. In 1930, when she was in high school, Winne was awarded the "Excellence in Food and Cookery" prize and received a hardcover book in which to record her recipes. Winnie's "Supper Dish" is one of those recipes.

Winne was known for her outstanding ability in the kitchen and especially for her homemade pies. She never failed to provide wonderful meals for her large family, as well as field hands working on the farm during the summer and fall harvests. She was a lifelong member of the Lynn Valley Women's Institute (WI) and held the organization in the highest esteem.

This is Winnie's recipe for a "Supper Dish." It is a simple layered potato and sausage casserole topped with a tin of tomato or mushroom soup, and then baked in the oven.

Sausage Casserole

A similar sausage casserole often cropped up in farm kitchens throughout Ontario, during the Great Depression, when casseroles became much more common. This change was in part due to the need to stretch expensive ingredients like meat, but also because electric ovens were becoming more commonplace. Old standby dishes like soups or stews that had simmered on the cast iron stovetops were being replaced by a new way of cooking.

Sausage casserole called for layers of thinly sliced potatoes and onions, topped with sliced carrots, tinned peas, a quarter cup of long grain rice, a layer of sausages, all topped off with a tin of tomato soup and a tin of water. The dish was baked covered in a moderate oven for about 45 minutes and then uncovered for another 15 minutes. Both dishes likely originated from the Dublin Coddle: a stew of potatoes, sausages, onion, seasonings, and bacon cooked in stock.

(Right) George Walker Collver and Allie Winnifred (Nelles) Collver, June 24, 1939, Bealton, ON]

Supper Dish

6 potatoes (pared & cored)
6 Sausages (boil in water 3 min & put in middle of potatoes).
Put in baking dish and pour over
1 can mushroom or tomato soup.
Season + bake until done.

---

9 Day Pickle

Put into strong cold brine 4 qts cucumber, small onions + cauliflower
Let stand 3 days then drain off the brine and place vegetables in good cold water for 3 day changing water daily.
Cook slowly in weak vinegar + water to which a very small piece of alum has been added for 1½ hrs then drain.
Boil together 2 qts vinegar, 4 lb brown sugar, 1 oz cinnamon, 1 oz allspice. Pour this over the pickles. Drain off the vinegar each day, bring to boil each day + again pour over pickles.

This is Winnie's recipe for a "Supper Dish." It is a simple layered potato and sausage casserole topped with a tin of tomato or mushroom soup, and then baked in the oven.

LADY DUFFERIN GOES FISHING

When Irish born, Hariot Georgina Rowan Hamilton married British aristocrat Lord Dufferin on October 23, 1862, she became formally known as Hariot, Marchioness of Dufferin and Ava or simply Lady Dufferin.

Lord Dufferin was appointed Governor General of Canada from 1872 to 1878. The couple brought with them their two youngest children, Hermione and Basil. The older children, Helen, Archibald, and Terence originally stayed in Britain, "trying to learn a little French. "Two more children, Victoria and Frederick, were born in Canada.

Lady Dufferin's weekly letters sent from Canada to her mother in Ireland later formed the basis of her book, *My Canadian Journal: 1872-1878*, in which Lady Dufferin revealed that she had spent some of her happiest times in Canada. The adventure, though, wasn't without its trials. She opens her memoir aboard the S.S. Prussian, en route to Canada:

"Friday, June 14th, 1872. – Ugh! Ugh! Horrid! Very rough, everybody ill except the wretched baby, Basil [her infant son], who is perfectly well, but can get no one to dress him, and is handed about, unwashed, to engineers, waiters, to anyone who can stand."

Thankfully the seas soon calmed, and Lady Dufferin was able to enjoy the remainder of her journey, as was the undaunted Basil. From the time she landed in Quebec City and throughout her years in Ontario, Lady Dufferin was much enamoured of Canada.

She proved remarkably adaptable, practical, incredibly well-natured, and game to try almost anything, especially if it involved the outdoors. Her writing is full of the delights of snowshoeing, fishing, skating, tobogganing, bonfires, yachting, and even camping. But it was fishing that really captured her imagination. She fished at every opportunity, sometimes getting up at five in the morning and fishing for four hours before breakfast and then returning to fish again in the evening.

"The gentleman were to go into the bush.... while we ladies were to fish… and caught fifty bass – a very good fresh water fish, and an amusing one to catch. We came home to lunch, sat two hours in the sunshine, and went out on the lake again in the afternoon," she wrote.

Lady Dufferin revelled in salmon fishing in particular. Sometimes she wrote about nothing but the fish:

Monday, 22nd [June 1874] – The salmon not rising… Tuesday, 23rd [June 1874] – Here are the statistics of our fishing so far at York River –
Mr. Reynolds, five fish [salmon] weighing 23, 21, 33, 28, 12 lbs.
Colonel McNeill, twelve, weighing 24, 22, 11, 18, 24, 25, 27, 25, 24, 20, 26, 14 lbs.
Mr. Monck, seven, weighing 25, 11, 26, 27, 27, 23, 15 lbs.
Lord D., three: 14, 13, 10 lbs.
Fred, two: 23, 14 lbs.

On the last day of August 1878, the Dufferin family bid farewell to Canada and Lady Dufferin made a final entry in her notes, including a goodbye to her "happy Canadian life," and ending with her sorrow at leaving, "...although the day was lovely, it was one of the most miserable I ever spent."

Fish were an important food source for both Indigenous Peoples and settlers. Fish were so plentiful in the early 1800s that one could dip a net into the water and pull out dinner or simply haul fish from the river with a garden rake.

Plenty of Fish

Whitefish were particularly abundant and prized for their rich, fine flavour. Families laid in enough fish to fill several barrels for winter and ice fishing was a popular winter pastime. Lakes and rivers supplied pike, pickerel, muskellunge, eels, whitefish, largemouth bass, mullet, lake herring, sturgeon, burbot, carp, shad, and wall-eye. Salmon, trout, perch, sunfish, and smallmouth bass were also plentiful. Salmon ran in the Don, Credit, and Humber rivers, amongst many others.

Fishing quickly became a lucrative industry and by the mid-1800s barrels of salted fish and fish packed in ice were shipped by boats and railroads into the United States. By 1867 there was a noticeable decline in the number of fish left and some fish populations were already close to being wiped out.

This planked fish recipe from the *Cook Book: Recipes Tested and Tried*, 1909, calls for a white-fleshed fish, but a salmon would work just as well. Soak the plank in water prior to cooking. Planked fish can be cooked filled with a sage, onion, and bread stuffing.

PLANKED FISH

For this select any white fleshed fish, a plank to fit oven at least an inch thick of hard wood. Rub the board with salt and make it hot, put the fish, skin side down, fold in thin parts dust with salt and pepper, let oven be hot at first then cook slowly for thirty minutes, have ready creamed potatoes and garnish fish with them, using pastry bag if you have it, garnish with sprigs of parsley, cuts of lemon, send to table at once (on plank.)   MRS. WEST.

Female Land Locked Salmon illustration 1896, by Sherman Foote Denton

FEMALE LAND LOCKED SALMON or OUANANICHE.
(Salmo Salar Sebago, Girard.)

A REVOLUTION IN THE KITCHEN

The introduction of the tin can, and hence, canned fruits and vegetables, canned milk, fish, and meat, was nothing short of a kitchen revolution. Canned goods meant access to tomatoes, corn, green beans, and peas in the middle of the harsh Canadian winter. It also meant the beginnings of liberation from relentless and endless work in the kitchen.

Imported canned goods began showing up in Upper Canada in the 1850s and 60s. The first cannery in Ontario is thought to have been established in 1870, in Picton, Prince Edward County, but fierce competition from the United States and an American import tariff on Canadian goods soon forced the closure of the province's first cannery.[34]

A Booming Industry is Born

By 1882, entrepreneur William Boulter had built a new canning factory in Picton and in short order he operated 75 canneries in the County. In 1902, Prince Edward County produced one third of Canada's canned goods. For almost exactly a century, the Ontario canning industry enjoyed a spectacular run before falling into decline.

Canned foods began to show up in Canadian cookbooks by the 1880s. Canned salmon was very popular and used in salads, moulds, croquettes, soup, salmon puddings, and salmon loaves.

Salmon Pudding.

Take the contents of one can of salmon, pound well and mix in a tablespoonful of butter; two eggs, half a cup of bread crumbs. Beat all well together, season with salt and pepper, press tightly into a pudding-mould and steam for an hour. Serve hot with white sauce.

Salmon Pudding (Salmon Loaf) from *The New Galt Cook Book*, 1898

A note about this recipe: salmon came in one pound (454 gram) cans. Two 213-gram cans would be a reasonable substitution. Salmon pudding was the precursor to salmon loaf: the only difference being the cooking method. Puddings were steamed. Loaves were baked. To make a salmon loaf, instead of steaming this in a pudding-mould, bake it in a buttered, loaf tin at 350°F for about 40 minutes or until set and lightly browned.

Three early canning labels from Prince Edward County, Ontario

CATHARINE PARR TRAILL'S WILD RICE PUDDING

Soon after Jell-O launched its flavoured and coloured gelatin products in Canada around 1906, it proclaimed itself to be "Canada's Favourite Dessert." Others begged to differ. Catharine Parr Traill, for example, once called Canada "the land of cakes."[35]

The truth is that Canada was also a land of puddings, pies, tarts, doughnuts, biscuits, squares and all manner of sweet things - the recipes for which were brought here by settlers, along with butter, sugar, and white flour.

Sweet Dishes

Indigenous Peoples had long used fruits, maple syrup, and maple sugar to sweeten dishes. They also used cornmeal and, for thousands of years, harvested and ate wild rice, or manomin, as it is known to the Ojibwa. Wild rice is a member of the grass family, indigenous to Ontario, and grows only in water.

In her book, *The Female Emigrant's Guide* (1854), Catharine Parr Traill suggested making wild rice into a pudding that could be served as either a sweet or savoury dish.

Wild-Rice Pudding

A basinful of Indian rice - carefully washed and picked, should be soaked for some hours; the water being poured off twice during that time. Put in on a covered vessel, with plenty of water, which should be drained off after it has boiled for half an hour, as there is a weedy, fishy taste with the rice, unless this is done. Milk may now be added in place of the water, with a little salt, and the rice simmered for an hour or more, till every grain has burst, and the milk is absorbed. Now add, when cool, four eggs, a bit of butter, sugar, and a little nutmeg or cinnamon. This makes an excellent baked or boiled pudding: and, leaving out the sugar, and spice, and eggs, and adding more salt, is a good vegetable dish.

Wild rice harvest sketch from, *The Female Emigrants Guide* **1854**

SETTLING THE NORTH

When Ignatius "Ned" Hummel (1855-1941) and his first wife, Joanna Weiler (1858-1882) moved north from New Germany (later renamed Maryhill), Waterloo Region, to the new township of South Himsworth in 1878, the land had only just been surveyed, and they were among the first settlers in the area.

Their daughter Catherine was the first child born in the settlement. Soon she was followed by another daughter, and then a son. But then tragedy struck, and Johanna Weiler died when she was just 24 years old, leaving Ned with three small children. Three years later, he married Rosina Rich (1864-1932) who bore fourteen children, including twins Rachel and Emma. In all, there were seventeen children in the Hummel family.

Gone for Groceries

For the first few years, the closest grocery story was twelve miles away in Commanda. Ned walked there to buy groceries, which he carried home on his back, making a 24-mile (40-kilometre) round trip. Once he went to buy flour only to find none available. He kept walking, all the way to Nipissing, another four hours through dense bush, forest, swamps, black flies, and mos-

Five of seventeen Hummel family siblings circa 1901
Front Row (L-R) Twins Regina "Rachel" and Emmaline "Emma" Hummel
Back Row (L-R) Catherine, Edward, and Hannah Hummel

quitoes on a road that was little more than a rough path over hills and rocky outcrops, and across streams. When he finally arrived in Nipissing, there was no flour in the store there either.

All he wanted was something nice for his two little girls to spare them from the rough diet the family were existing on, likely salt pork and root vegetables. The only thing the shopkeeper could offer was soda biscuits, so Ned bought those and made the long trek back home, a 38.5-mile (62-kilometre) round trip.

Another couple who moved to the South Himsworth area around the same time spent their first winter living on nothing but turnips and potatoes. In time the families found each other and became much-needed support systems in the wilderness of the "Near North."

Boomtown

In the mid 1880s, the Northern and Pacific Railway ran a line heading north from Gravenhurst to North Bay. Soon the Grand Trunk Railway purchased the rail line and by 1892, the village of Trout Creek was established, and a train station was built. More settlers began arriving, drawn by the prospects of work in the booming lumber industry and lured by the talk of using local rivers for power generation.

A water tower, sawmill, butcher shop, watchmakers shop, grocery stores, churches, a hall, many new homes, and three hotels were erected. Almost overnight Trout Creek became a boomtown, a place where lumberjacks and railway workers came to spend their earnings in the hotels. But also a place where Ned and Rosina's children finally had a school to attend.

A Dynasty

In 1918, Ned and Rosina Hummel's 22-year-old daughter, Rachel Hummel, married John George Lang and the couple went on to have 11 children. Rachel's sixteen siblings also married and had families, and many stayed in Northern Ontario, keeping alive the Hummel dynasty.

The qualities Ned and Rosina Hummel passed down – stoicism, kindness, integrity, faith, and a relentless work ethic – are found in the generations that followed, many of whom still live in the area to this day.

Photograph of Trout Creek, circa 1900

Rachel Hummel's Strawberry Sherbet

From her manuscript cookbook written in the elegant cursive that she no doubt practiced at school, this is Rachel Hummel Lang's recipe for strawberry sherbet.

Strawberry Sherbet

1 quart of berries
1 ½ cups sugar
1 cup water
½ lemon

Mash berries through a sieve. Make syrup of sugar and water. [Bring the sugar and water to a boil and stir to dissolve sugar.] Add [juice of] lemon when cold. Add berries and freeze.

Mayonnaise Dressing

Beat yolks of 2 eggs add drop
by drops of ¾ cup olive oil beat
oil only cold ½ teaspoon salt
shake of cyenne pepper level
1 teaspoons mustard
1 " pwd sugar
2 tablespoons lemon juice
4 " " viniger, have all very cold

Salad Dressing
1 table spoon B. sugar 1 teaspoon mustard
1 " Butter
2 egg pinch of salt
1 tablespoon flour
1 " " viniger pinch of pepper
let boil over kettle, stir till smooth

"Salts of Lemon is good to clean Hats"

Straw Berry Sherbet
1 qt of Berries
1½ cup sugar
1 " water
½ lemon. Mash berries through a
sieve make a syrup of sugar &
water add lemon when cold add
Berries and Freeze.

Jelly Roll.
¾ cup sugar
1 " flour
3 eggs 1 teaspoon cream of tartar
½ teaspoon cream of tartar ½ teas

Manuscript Cookbook of Rachel (Hummel) Lang

CHARLOTTE RUSSE D'ERABLE

My father was English and even after decades in Canada, he still had a Yorkshire accent, though he denied it vehemently. He loved Canada, his adopted homeland. He loved the history, the wild and expansive landscape, the opportunity, and the freedom from the class system.

He was tall, thin, wiry, driven – a weekday engineer and a mad-keen weekend hiker and mountaineer, a lover of the North, the Great Lakes, the heritage rivers, and the stories of the building of a nation. The only thing he ever missed, surprisingly enough, was English cooking. Especially dessert. Steamed, stodgy puddings like jam roly-poly, treacle pudding, or Spotted Dick.

What's for Pud?

Each night he crashed through the door after work practically shouting, "What's for pud?" The universal term he applied to dessert. He was never happier than when there was a homemade apple pie, or a steamed ginger pudding with custard, or any one of his many boyhood favourites. But this dessert – a Canadianized version of Charlotte Russe – also won him over.

Charlotte Russe is a party dessert: elegant, light, and sophisticated but surprisingly simple. It was immensely popular in the Victorian era. Made with sweetened whipped cream, set with gelatin, and served in a ring of savoy biscuits or lady fingers, it was invented in France, by Chef Marie-Antoine Carême (1784-1833). Carême named the dish to honour Princess Charlotte, the daughter of his former employer, King George IV; and his employer at the time, Alexander I, Emperor of Russia.

Almost every early Canadian cookbook included at least one recipe for Charlotte Russe, and some listed several versions.

Maple Syrup

By the early 1900s, recipes for Charlotte Russe-type desserts using maple syrup in place of granulated sugar were cropping up in Canadian cookbooks. *Culinary Landmarks of Sault Ste. Marie* (1909) included a Maple Bisque that was essentially a Charlotte Russe made with maple syrup sans ladyfingers. And in 1924, Nellie Lyle Pattinson's *Canadian Cook Book* included a Maple Mousse that was identical to the recipe below, but also minus the ladyfingers.

When my family moved to Canada, my mother acquired this recipe for Charlotte Russe d'erable. This became one of her go-to dinner party recipes. The first time she served it my father dubbed it, "tombstone torte," because the ladyfingers around the edge looked like gravestones. I never knew it by any other name.

Charlotte Russe d'Erable

1 envelope unflavoured gelatin
¼ cup cold water
1 cup hot maple syrup
1-pint (2 cups or 473 ml) whipping cream, firmly whipped and refrigerated to stay cold
¼ cup crushed walnuts to garnish

Lightly grease a 9-inch (23 x 8cm) springform pan.

Combine the gelatin and cold water and let stand two or three minutes to soften. Stir in the hot maple syrup. Set aside to cool. When mixture begins to thicken, gently stir in the whipped cream.

Line the edge of the pan with ladyfingers, bottom side of the fingers facing in, good sides facing out. Use remaining ladyfingers (as many as required) to line the base of the pan.

Spoon the whipped cream/maple mixture into the lined springform pan. Refrigerate until firm. Sprinkle with crushed walnuts. Remove from springform pan and plate.

Charlotte Russe D'Erable aka Tombstone Torte from my mother's kitchen. Approximately 30-35 small ladyfingers (packaged or make your own.

Puddings: *Mrs. Beeton's Every Day Cookery and Housekeeping,* 1893

Open Apple Tart.

Galette.

Iced Pudding.

Apricot Fritters.

Pancakes & Apricot Jam.

Macaroni Cheese.

Charlotte Russe.

Cherry Tart.

Mince Pies.

Almond Puddings.

Tartlets.

Compote of Fruits.

Fruit Pudding.

Fruit Tart.

Christmas Plum Pudding.

Milk Pudding.

Roly Poly Jam Pudding.

PUDDINGS & PASTRY.

ISABELLA LUCY BIRD DISCOVERS THE SECRET OF APPLE DUMPLINGS

Isabella Lucy Bird Bishop, (1831-1904) born in Yorkshire, England, was an early travel writer, an intrepid and courageous global explorer, a photographer, and naturalist. She was the first woman ever to be elected a Fellow of the Royal Geographical Society, and along with Dr. Fanny Jane Butler, co-founded the John Bishop Memorial Hospital in Srinagar, Kashmir.

Because she was frail and unwell as a child, Isabella was homeschooled by her mother, Dora Lawson and father, Edward Bird, an Anglican minister. Her unorthodox education included lessons in botany, riding, rowing, language, and critical thinking. When the local Member of Parliament called at the house campaigning, six-year-old Isabella asked him, "Sir Malpas de Grey Tatton Egerton, did you tell my father my sister was so pretty because you wanted his vote?"[36]

A Writing Career Takes Off

At age 16, Isabella published her first written work, a pamphlet on the topic of free trade versus protectionism. And thus her writing career was born. She went on to write many articles and several books.

At age 19, Isabella had a major tumorous growth removed from the vicinity of her spine. Her recovery afterwards was slow. After a couple of years of difficulty, her doctors prescribed a sea voyage.

Her father gave her 100 pounds and soon after Isabella set off aboard a Cunard Line royal mail steamer, bound for North America. Her trip through Eastern Canada, including present day Ontario and the United States, set off a passion for travelling that would eventually see her traverse the globe. In Canada West (Ontario), Isabella visited Niagara, the Burlington Bay area, Hamilton (where she stopped in at Dundurn Castle), Ancaster, Dundas, and Toronto.

She spent a month with the Forrest family at their home in the backwoods of Upper Canada. They drove for many miles through the autumn forest in all its glory. "There all my dreams of Canadian scenery were more than realized," Isabella wrote, "Trees grew in every variety of the picturesque."

Isabella apparently settled happily into her temporary life in the Ontario backwoods: "The way of life at Mr. Forrest's was peculiarly agreeable," she wrote. "The breakfast hour was nominally seven, and afterwards, Mr. Forrest went out to his farm. The one Irish servant, who never seemed happy with her shoes on, was capable of little else than boiling potatoes, so all the preparations for dinner devolved upon Mrs. Forrest, who when she came to Canada had never attempted anything in the culinary line. I used to accompany her into the kitchen, and learned how to solve the problem which puzzled an English king, viz. 'How apples get into a dumpling.'"[37]

Apple Dumplings
NB. Adjust cooking temperature to 350°F or 180°C

(Right) Apple Dumplings from an unknown newspaper advertisement circa 1930s

Apple Dumplings

1 quart flour	1½ cups milk
2 teaspoons Magic Baking Powder	Sugar
½ teaspoon salt	Cinnamon
2 tablespoons butter	Apples

Sift into a bowl flour, baking powder and salt. Rub in the butter. Add cold milk to make soft dough. Turn out on to a floured board and roll into a sheet. Cut in squares. Peel and core the apples. Place an apple on each square of dough. Fill the core with a small piece of butter, sugar and a little cinnamon. Fold the dough over, taking care that there are no openings, as the steam inside dumpling cooks the apple while dough is baking. Brush dumplings with a little cream, and place in greased pans. Bake in moderate oven at 400° F. about 40 minutes. Serve with cream or hard sauce.

Tested and Approved by
Chatelaine Institute
Chatelaine Magazine

MAGIC BAKING POWDER

THE WHITEST LIGHT I.L.B.

CONTAINS NO ALUM

"CONTAINS NO ALUM." This statement on every tin is your guarantee that Magic Baking Powder is free from alum or any harmful ingredient.

Made in Canada

FREE COOK BOOK—When you bake at home, the new Magic Cook Book will give you dozens of recipes for delicious baked foods. Write to Standard Brands Ltd., Fraser Ave. & Liberty St., Toronto, Ont.

THE ESSENTIAL PLUM PUDDING

Plum pudding has its roots in medieval English cooking, when there were few ways to preserve other than drying, salting, or fermenting. Dried fruits, including raisins, prunes, figs, currants, and apricots, were an important commodity in a time when sugar was an expensive luxury item. Dried fruits also served as a preservative of sorts in many households, where the only sugar to be had was that contained in fruits.

Christmas Plum Pudding, Mrs. Beeton

In its earliest origins, plum pudding contained ground meat as well as suet, grains, spices, salt and whatever dried fruits were on hand. This mixture, a cross between sausage and haggis, would have been encased in animal bladders or intestines for storage.

Only later, when sugar became more commonplace, did the more contemporary version of plum pudding (without meat) make an appearance. The same is true for mince pie.

The Pudding King

Plum pudding's noble lineage was cemented in 1714, when a German from Hanover became the King of England. King George I, also known as the Pudding King, is said to have requested plum pudding for his first Christmas dinner in England. German-speaking George was an unpopular king when he arrived, initially speaking very little English.

But he had one particularly endearing characteristic: he loved food and sharing it with others. He was the first king to be seen dining in public places and he held massive feasts and balls at Hampton Court, sometimes several times a week, using food and alcohol as a way to win over the British.

By the Victorian era, plum pudding was a firmly entrenched British tradition. It had the virtuous benefit of being an egalitarian dish because although cast iron stoves had begun to appear in the most affluent households, the plum pudding being steamed and not baked, did not require the luxury of owning an oven.

King George I by Sir Godfrey Kneller

Around the Globe

In 1927, the British Empire Marketing Board wrote to the royal household, requesting a copy of the Royal Family's Christmas pudding recipe. The recipe was scaled and ingredients from each of the colonies were included: brandy from Cyprus, nutmeg from the West Indies, Australian currants, South African raisins, Jamaican rum, English beer, and Canadian apples. Thousands of copies of that recipe were circulated, making the plum pudding popular all over again.

THE EMPIRE CHRISTMAS PUDDING

according to the recipe supplied by the King's Chef Mr. CEDARD, with Their Majesties' Gracious Consent

1 lb	Currants	Australia
1 lb	Sultanas	Australia or South Africa
1 lb	Stoned Raisins	Australia or South Africa
5 ozs	Minced Apple	United Kingdom or Canada
1 lb	Bread Crumbs	United Kingdom
1 lb	Beef Suet	United Kingdom
6½ ozs	Cut Candied Peel	South Africa
8 ozs	Flour	United Kingdom
8 ozs	Demerara Sugar	British West Indies or British Guiana
5	Eggs	United Kingdom or Irish Free State
½ oz	Ground Cinnamon	India or Ceylon
¼ oz	Ground Cloves	Zanzibar
¼ oz	Ground Nutmegs	British West Indies
¼ teaspoon	Pudding Spice	India or British West Indies
¼ gill	Brandy	Australia · S. Africa Cyprus or Palestine
½ gill	Rum	Jamaica or British Guiana
1 pint	Beer	England · Wales · Scotland or Ireland

WRITE TO THE EMPIRE MARKETING BOARD, WESTMINSTER, FOR A FREE BOOKLET ON EMPIRE CHRISTMAS FARE GIVING THIS AND OTHER RECIPES.

A Simple Plum Pudding

This simple recipe, from *Ogilvie's Book for a Cook*, produces a smaller plum pudding requiring less suet. If in doubt about using suet, shortening, lard, or butter can be used in its place. Serve with rum butter (recipe below), brandy sauce, or custard.

PLUM PUDDING

2 cups "Ogilvie's Royal Household" Flour

½ cup suet, chopped fine.
½ cup brown sugar.
½ cup molasses.
½ cup water.
½ teaspoon salt.
½ teaspoon soda.
2 teaspoons baking powder.
2 eggs.

1 teaspoon cinnamon.
½ teaspoon nutmeg.
¼ teaspoon allspice.
¼ cup citron peel.
2 tablespoons candied orange peel.
½ cup raisins.
½ cup currants.

CUT raisins; cut peel into thin slices; add currants and sprinkle all with part of the flour.

Remove membrane from suet; chop finely.

Sift all the dry ingredients.

Mix together the suet, molasses and water; add the well-beaten eggs; then the prepared fruit.

Add the sifted dry ingredients gradually, beating after each addition.

Pour into greased mould and steam 3 or 4 hours, or into smaller moulds and steam 2 or 3 hours.

Note:—If using an ordinary steamer and an uncovered mould, cover with heavy waxed paper or greased brown paper, leaving plenty of room for pudding to rise.

Variations:—¼ cup of blanched chopped almonds and ¼ cup candied cherries (cut).

Rum Butter

225 grams or 1 cup salted butter at room temperature
1 cup brown sugar
8 tbsp amber or dark rum

Using a hand-held mixer, beat the butter and brown sugar for several minutes. Add the rum, slowly, and keep beating until it is fully incorporated. Store in a sealed glass jar in the refrigerator. If the rum separates, don't worry, just give it a good stir prior to using. Serve with plum pudding, mince tarts, apple crisp, or a tart apple pie.

LUELLA ERB'S POOR MAN'S PUDDING

Luella (Buzzard) Erb (1907-1987) was the tenth of twelve children born into a Mennonite farm family in Waterloo County. An accident when she was a baby resulted in one of her legs being shorter than the other and as a consequence she walked with a significant limp. Her parents assumed that that handicap would prevent Luella from doing many things including marrying, so she was trained young to cook in the hopes that she might stay home and cook and care for her aging parents.

A Feast from Nothing

Luella was undeterred and never once let her handicap stand in her way. She donned her long floral apron and became an exceptional cook who could make a feast from next to nothing.

Whether it was egg noodles filled with seasoned bread dressing simmering in beef broth; fork tender, slow-cooked pork chops simmered in a cast iron skillet; homemade chicken soup with "pigs" (dense egg noodles); or her mother, Magdalena Buzzard's elderberry pie (recipe appears later) – she turned out meal after meal of hearty, beautiful, delicious food. And despite the odds, she also married and had a family of her own.

This is Luella's simple, delicious Poor Man's Pudding recipe (later versions of this pudding were often called Half Hour Pudding or Hasty Pudding). Sometimes there were no raisins or dates in the pantry, but even without them, the baked self-saucing pudding is just as delicious. The recipe is still a family favourite, five generations on.

Poor Man's Pudding

Batter:
½ cup brown sugar
½ cup raisins or dates (may be omitted)
½ cup milk or water
2 tsp baking powder

Sauce:
2 cups boiling water
1 cup brown sugar
1 tbsp butter

Butter a round Pyrex or similar bowl. Mix the batter ingredients together and spoon into the prepared dish. Mix the sauce ingredients together and pour over the batter. Bake in a moderate oven (350°F or 175°C) until browned, or about 45 minutes.

CHOCOLATE FUDGE UPSIDE DOWN PUDDING

Mary (Allen Clark) Moore, born in Hamilton in 1903, was a nationally syndicated Canadian food columnist whose stories appeared in as many as 25 daily newspapers from the 1930s to the 1970s. Mary studied home economics and journalism before she married Henry F. Moore in 1924. When their marriage broke down in 1942, Mary was left to raise their two children, Marianne and Peter.

Mary Moore's first column was a St. Patrick's Day food story in a special supplement to the *Edmonton Journal*. Mary and her sisters, Pearl and Doris, also ran a canning factory under the brand name Mary Miles.

Corn Syrup Instead of Sugar

During the Second World War, the St. Lawrence Starch Company asked Mary Moore to develop recipes using Bee Hive Corn Syrup as a sweetener due to the sugar rationing. After creating various recipes, Mary took her sample to feed the Bee Hive company president and staff. They offered her $1,200 and three weeks to come up with a booklet of recipes using Bee Hive Corn Syrup instead of sugar. With the help of her sisters, Mary managed to meet her deadline and used the money as a down payment for a home in Hamilton.

When the war ended, Mary continued to write her heartwarming, highly personal columns with recipes and cooking advice. She encouraged her readers to try new dishes and take a long walk each day. Her recipe flops were just part of her charm.

Very close to the end of her life, in 1978, she produced a cookbook of her favourite recipes entitled *The Mary Moore Cookbook*, in which she described the pleasure she had derived from her family, readers and friends.

Mary Moore's column including a reader's recipe for a baked, self-saucing Chocolate Fudge Upside Down Pudding follows.

Upside down pudding

Conducted By Mary Moore

LETTER: I am sending a recipe for a chocolate self-saucing pudding which uses cocoa. Mrs. A. M. K.

ANSWER: My secretary Betty tested your pudding Mrs. K. and when we tasted it we liked the true fudge flavor. The fact that it calls for cocoa instead of unsweetened chocolate will appeal to all budget watchers.

CHOCOLATE FUDGE UPSIDE DOWN PUDDING (no eggs; courtesy Mrs. A. M. K.: serves 6)

Batter:

- ¾ cup granulated sugar (first amount)
- 2 tablespoons margarine
- ½ cup milk
- 1 cup unsifted all-purpose flour
- 2 teaspoons baking powder
- ¼ teaspoon salt
- 2 tablespoons cocoa (first amount)
- ½ cup chopped walnuts

Topping:

- ½ cup granulated sugar (second amount)
- ½ cup brown sugar
- 1-3 cup cocoa (second amount)
- 1½ cups boiling water

To make the batter in mixing bowl cream together the sugar (first amount) and the margarine until creamy then stir in the milk. Over the creamed mixture sift together the flour, baking powder, salt and cocoa and stir in until batter is smooth. Add and stir in walnuts. Turn into greased 8 x 8" square pan.

To make topping in a small bowl mix together thoroughly the white and brown sugars and the cocoa and sprinkle evenly over the top of batter. Now slowly with a back and forth motion, pour the boiling water all over the top. Bake at 350 deg. Fahr. 30 to 40 minutes. The wide spread in our suggested timing is because Mrs. K. suggests 35 to 40 minutes, but Betty's pudding was baked in a gas oven in 30 minutes. So since this is rich with sugar you must watch it to be sure it is removed from oven before it has a chance to burn on bottom.

Serve warm with whole milk if desired.

Whig-Standard Pattern

PRINTED PATTERN

4526
SIZES
10½-18½

by Anne Adams

SLEEKEST CUT OF ALL is the cardigan swooping down, down a track traced by top stitching and princess lines. Choose blends, knits.

Printed Pattern 4526: NEW Half Sizes 10½, 12½, 14½, 16½, 18½. Size 14½ (bust 37) takes 26 yards 39-inch fabric.

SEVENTY - FIVE CENTS (75c) in coins (no stamps, please) for each pattern — add 15 cents for each pattern for first-class mailing and special handling. Ontario residents add 4c sales tax. Print plainly SIZE, NAME, ADDRESS, STYLE NUMBER.

Send order to ANNE ADAMS, Whig-Standard Pattern Dept. 60 Front Street West, Toronto 1.

NEW - NOW! SPRING-SUMMER Pattern Catalogue. 111 styles, free pattern coupon. 50c. INSTANT SEWING BOOK — cut, fit, sew modern way. $1.00. INSTANT FASHION BOOK — wardrobe planning secrets, flattery, accessory tips. $1.00.

EGG IN MEAT LOAF

Home economists, Macdonald Institute, University of Guelph, say that a hard-cooked egg baked whole in the centre of your favorite meat loaf adds an attractive difference to each serving, as well as important nutrients.

From the *Kingston Whig-Standard*, date unknown

COBBLERS, CRUMBLES, GRUNTS, CRISPS, AND BETTYS

Fruit cobblers, crumbles, grunts, crisps, and brown Bettys all originated in the British colonies in the mid to late 1800s, in part, it is thought, because ingredients for traditional British steamed puddings were less easy to come by than fresh fruit, sugar, butter, flour, oatmeal, cornmeal, and breadcrumbs – ingredients usually used in these baked fruit desserts.

Apple Brown Betty typically called for sweetened bread crumbs, mixed with butter, and layers of apples. Crisps or crumbles ('crumble' was the British term, 'crisp' the American term, and both were used in Canada) were usually made with a mixture of flour, oatmeal, butter, and sugar. Cobblers tended to have a tea-biscuit type topping. Grunts and slumps were more common in the Maritime Provinces and the United States and involved stewed or cooked fruit topped with tea biscuits or a tea-biscuit crust.

From Yorkshire

My mother made a spectacular Christmas crumble that came from an ancient Yorkshire cookbook. She used a half a large jar of Cross & Blackwell mincemeat (the other half was used to make mince tarts), mixed with peeled, chopped apples, and a variety of other fruits according to what she had on hand.

The recipe became Canadianized once she moved here. She added a couple of handfuls of fresh or frozen cranberries, and whatever other fruit was in the freezer, often blueberries, blackberries, peaches, and rhubarb. She mixed the topping by memory with quantities varying according to the amount of fruit she had used. Here's my rendition of my mother's very old recipe for Yorkshire Christmas Crumble.

Christmas Crumble

2 cups commercial or homemade mincemeat
3 or 4 cooking apples such as MacIntosh, peeled, cored, and chopped
1 cup fresh or frozen cranberries
1 cup fresh or frozen rhubarb chopped
1 cup fresh or frozen blueberries or chopped peaches or whatever other fruit is on hand

Topping:
1 cup all purpose flour
1 cup quick cooking oats
1 cup brown sugar
½ cup butter
½ tsp salt

Mix the mincemeat and other fruits together and spread in a 9 x 13 inch (23 x 33cm) buttered glass baking dish.
Mix together the flour, oats, brown sugar, and salt. Cut in the butter until the mixture is crumbly and the butter is distributed throughout. Sprinkle the crumble mixture on top of the fruit. Bake at 325°F (165°C) for 35-45 minutes or until golden brown. Serve hot, warm, or cold with whipped cream or rum butter.

Tab. 78.

Sambucus nigra L. b. Fructus.

Elderberry botanical drawing 1828-1830

A Classic Mennonite Elderberry Pie

Magdalena (Gerber) Buzzard (1871-1959) came from a Swiss-German Mennonite family that found its way to a farm in Waterloo County. Her great-granddaughter, Deborah Cardiff, herself a grand-mother now, remembers Magdalena as a very kind, elderly woman, who had long white hair that fell to her waist. When she was up and around, her hair was worn tightly twisted into a small bun and covered with a Mennonite prayer covering. Only when she was quite elderly and receiving family visitors in her bedroom, perched on her high bed, was her beautiful long white hair left loose.

Magdalena, a busy farm wife and mother of twelve, was a notoriously good cook. Six generations on, her elderberry pie recipe, made from wild elderberries picked along the fence lines in Waterloo County, is still in use in the family. These days, the elderberries are often purchased from Waterloo County markets.

Elderberries are not lucrative enough to be a commercial crop, but elderberry bushes can easily be grown in home gardens. The fruit can be used in pies, jams, jellies, and wine. The plant is an attractive fruit bearing bush, with beautiful, fragrant blossoms.

Magdalena Buzzard's Elderberry Pie

As adapted by her descendants

Pastry for a double crust pie
4-5 cups elderberries
1 cup sugar
Pinch of cinnamon
½ cup water

Handful of flour to hold berries together while cooking

Mix the washed, sorted elderberries with the sugar, cinnamon, water, and handful of flour.

Check for sweetness and add a little more sugar if necessary.

Fill the unbaked pie crust with berry mixture.

Add the top crust and brush with milk and sprinkle with sugar. 'Kringle' the pie crust edges together and using a knife, cut slits in the shape of a Christmas tree, in order for the pie to vent while cooking.

Bake at 350°F (175°C) until crust is golden brown and berry mixture is bubbling, about 45-60 minutes.

Magdalena (2nd row centre) and to her left, husband, Jonas Buzzard, with their twelve children, circa 1919

Mary, Loretta, Magdalena, Elmira (Minnie) and Luella sitting on a rug they have just finished making, circa 1924

Mock Cherry Pie

Pastry for a double-crust pie
1½ cups cranberries
1½ cups raisins
1 cup white sugar
1 tbsp flour
[¼ tsp salt]
1 tbsp vanilla

Cook the cranberries, raisins, sugar, [salt], and flour together until thick. Add vanilla. Spoon into pastry shell. Cover with upper crust. Bake.

Fresh Strawberry Pie

One prebaked pie crust
1-quart strawberries
1 – 1½ cups sugar
2 tbsp flour
¼ tsp salt

Whipped cream to serve
Gently mash strawberries, salt, and sugar together [in a saucepan]. Put on the stove and bring to boil. Add 2 tbsp flour dissolved in a little cold water and stir until mixture thickens. Pour onto crust. Let stand to cold. Serve with slightly sweetened whipped cream.

(Top Left) Mock Cherry Pie from the *Zion Cook Book*, (Kingston) circa 1929

(Top Right) Fresh Strawberry Pie adapted slightly from *Ogilvie's Book for a Cook*, 1931

(Bottom) Sour Cream Raisin Pie adapted slightly from *The Alexandra Club Cook Book*, 1952

Sour Cream Raisin Pie

[unbaked single pie crust]
1 cup sour cream
1 cup brown sugar
1 cup raisins
2 eggs separated
½ tsp cinnamon, cloves, and nutmeg
Dash salt

Combine the sour cream, brown sugar, raisins, egg yolks, salt, and spices. Beat egg whites until stiff and add to the raisin mixture. Pour into the pie crust and cook in at 375°F/190°C until filling is set and pastry is nicely browned (about 40 minutes). [Egg whites may be whipped with 3 tbsp white sugar and used a meringue, instead of mixing with filling. In which case, add the meringue about 10 minutes before the end of the cooking time and continue cooking until meringue is browned.]

Butterscotch Pie

½ cup flour
1 cup light brown sugar
½ tsp salt
2 ¾ cups milk, scalded
2 egg yolks, well-beaten
3 tbsp butter
1 tsp vanilla

1 baked 9-inch pie shell
Meringue
3 tbsp sugar
¼ tsp salt
2 egg whites, stiffly beaten

Mix flour, brown sugar and salt in top of a double boiler.

Add milk gradually and cook in double boiler until thickened, stirring constantly.

Pour small amount of mixture over egg yolks, stirring vigorously.

Return [egg mixture] to double boiler, add butter, and cook three minutes, stirring constantly.

Add vanilla, cool. Pour into [pre-baked] pie shell, cover with meringue [beat egg whites to stiff, slowly beat in sugar and salt] and brown under slow oven [300°F/150°C] for 10-12 minutes.

Rhubarb Pie

Two cups of fresh rhubarb cut into small pieces, one tablespoon cornstarch, one cup of sugar, yolks of three eggs, a small piece of butter. Mix well together, put into pie. Bake crust and filling together. Put beaten whites on top and brown.

(Top) Butterscotch Pie from the 1933 Canada Packers Limited cookbook, *Tasty Meal for Every Day*

(Above) Rhubarb Custard Meringue Pie from *The Toronto Cook Book*, 1915*

*This is a delicious rhubarb custard pie! Use 3 cups of chopped rhubarb instead of the 2 cups the recipe calls for and 2 tbsp of cornstarch instead of 1. And be sure to add some sugar to the beaten egg whites to make the meringue — ¼ cup should be plenty. Bake the pie at 400°F for 20 minutes then reduce temperature to 325°F and cook another 20 minutes or until custard is set. Then remove the pie from oven, add the meringue, and return the pie to the oven until the meringue is lightly browned. Let the pie stand several hours, until fully cooled, before cutting and serving.

Economy Recipes
FOR
CANADA'S "HOUSOLDIERS"

HOME SERVICE DEPARTMENT
THE CANADA STARCH COMPANY LIMITED — MONTREAL — TORONTO

UPPER CANADA GETS A NEW APPLE

The origin of the humble but wildly popular McIntosh apple, has been largely credited to John McIntosh and his wife Hannah, who in 1811 found the apples growing on their farm in Matilda Township (renamed South Dundas Township), just north of the St. Lawrence River between Gananoque and Cornwall.

John McIntosh (1777–1846) was born in the Province of New York to Scottish parents. A Loyalist, McIntosh emigrated to Canada around 1796 and was married to Hannah Doran (Dorin) in 1801. The couple had six sons and five daughters.

An Apple A Day

In 1811, in the bush on the family farm, John McIntosh discovered a number of seedling apple trees growing, believed to have derived from the Snow apple. McIntosh transplanted the trees with small success but by 1835, his son, Allan McIntosh, having learned about grafting, began producing apples on a larger scale. By 1870 the McIntosh apple was a huge commercial success and remains one of the most popular North American apple cultivars to this day.

Apples were an important source of food for settlers. During the 1800s, there were more than seven thousand named varieties of apples grown in North America. Today only about 300 of those original varieties exist and a mere handful of apples make up most of the market share. Red Delicious apples alone account for over one third of all apples grown.[38]

Apples were used to make cider, cakes, pies, apple butter, chutneys, apple sauce, and apple puddings. Those apples that stored well were barrelled in the autumn. Others were sliced and dried and then used reconstituted. Dried apples were known as "sarce." Dried apples, like raisins, were particularly useful by late winter and spring when little else in the way of fruit was available.

"The drying of apples is a great business in the houses of Canadian farmers where they have orchards, or live near those who have large orchards, who will sell the inferior fruit very cheap…" wrote Catharine Parr Traill in *The Female Emigrant's Guide*. "Bushels and bushels of apples are pared, cored and strung on Dutch thread, by the young men and maidens, and the walls of the kitchen are festooned round with the apples, where they hang till dry and shrivelled. They should be dipped into boiling water as they are hung up; this preserves the colour…. When required for use, they are steeped for some time in hot water."

Drying apples is a lot faster in a dehydrator. Or if, like me, you're short of space and desire for extra kitchen appliances, wash, core, peel, and slice your apples horizontally into thin rings and place them on baking sheets in the oven at the lowest possible heat setting. Check the apples at about two hours. They can take up to about four hours but you'll want to keep an eye on them. They should be drying rather than cooking. After about three or four hours you can turn the oven off and leave the apples for several more hours to use up any residual heat.

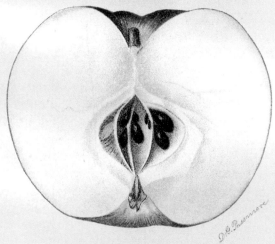

MC INTOSH APPLE.

McIntosh Apple botanical illustration, by Deborah Griscom Passmore, 1901

Dried Apple Cake

This delicious, moist, spicy, flavourful cake is adapted (and halved) from the original version in the *Canadian Farm Cook Book*, 1911. A similar version appears in *The Home Cook Book*, 1877. You can also make it with fresh cooking apples, peeled and finely chopped, in which case, just warm the molasses and add the chopped apples instead of cooking the mixture for half an hour. It won't be quite as intensely flavourful but it is still a beautiful, rich cake. Serve with whipped cream.

Dried Apple Cake

1 cup of dried apples (soaked overnight) or 2 cups fresh cooking apples peeled and chopped
1 cup fancy molasses
1 egg, beaten
½ cup sugar
½ cup buttermilk or soured milk
¼ cup butter, softened
1 tsp baking soda
2 cups all-purpose flour
1 tsp cinnamon
½ tsp dried ginger
½ tsp allspice
Pinch salt

Soak apples overnight in water. Drain and chop lightly.

Simmer in molasses for about 30 minutes. Allow to cool.

In a separate bowl, beat the egg, sugar, buttermilk, and butter.

Stir well. Add the flour, baking soda, spices, and salt.

Stir in the apple mixture. Combine well.

Pour into a well-greased ring cake pan or bundt cake pan. Bake at 325 for about 45 minutes or until the cake springs back lightly when touched.

Allow to cool in pan before removing. Serve with vanilla ice cream and/or whipped cream.

ADELAIDE HOODLESS: EDUCATIONAL REFORMER AND EARLY FEMALE ACTIVIST

When 14-month-old John Harold Hoodless died in 1889, likely from causes related to drinking contaminated milk, his mother, Adelaide Hoodless, started a quiet revolution – a new era of female activism.

Addie (Hunter) Hoodless (1857- 1910) was born on a farm in St George, County Brant, Canada West. She was the youngest of 12 children. When her father died within months of her birth, Addie's mother, Jane Hamilton Hunter, had not only to cope with singlehandedly raising her large family, but also had to manage the farm and generate an income. Adelaide Hoodless's own determination and strength were likely inherited but also learned from watching her hardworking and immensely capable mother.

Adelaide Hunter married John Hoodless in 1881 and the couple moved to Hamilton, where they soon had four children: Edna, Muriel, Bernard, and John Harold. When their infant son John Harold died, the death certificate listed meningitis as the cause of his death, though Adelaide believed the infection stemmed from drinking unpasteurized milk. These were the days before refrigeration, and pasteurization was relatively new and not yet in widespread use.

Adelaide Hunter Hoodless, oil painting by Marion Long

A Movement Rises from Tragedy

Immediately following her son's death, a devastated Adelaide Hoodless began working to prevent the similar deaths of others by providing and reforming education for young women. By 1890 she was president of the Young Women's Christian Association (YWCA) of Hamilton and used her role to establish domestic science education.

By 1895, she had founded the Canadian National YWCA. She was also a co-founder along with Sir William Macdonald of the Macdonald Institute at the University of Guelph, which opened in 1903. Along with Lady Aberdeen, wife of the Governor General, Adelaide Hoodless helped to found the National Council of Women and the Victorian Order of Nurses, which provided nursing to the poor.

Hoodless travelled throughout Ontario lecturing, educating, and speaking on the topic of domestic science. By all accounts she was a captivating speaker and although she was not a suffragist she was an early advocate for female education and the recognition of the importance of traditional female roles.

Not to be Under Estimated

"Is it of greater importance that a farmer should know more about the scientific care of his sheep and cattle, than a farmer's wife should know how to care for her family?" she asked, emphasizing in a time before childcare or any suggestion of gender parity, that raising a family was important work not to be underestimated.

In 1897, when Adelaide was asked to speak at a Farmers Institute Ladies Night, she proposed forming a women's group to socialize and share knowledge of domestic science and agriculture. One week later, the group had gone from a mere suggestion to being 101 women strong. Adelaide Hoodless was onto something: women wanted to connect and share knowledge.

From these humble beginnings the Women's Institute, now an international organization, got its start. Within a decade there were 500 branches across Canada and Adelaide Hoodless was appointed the organization's honorary president.

The Little Red Book

In 1898, on the invitation of Ontario's Minister of Education, Adelaide Hoodless published a cooking and home economics textbook titled *Public School Domestic Science*, which quickly became known as the Little Red Book. The following recipes for gingerbread cake and accompanying sauces are taken from the Little Red Book pages, exactly as they first appeared.

Gingerbread.

1 cup molasses.
2 tbsps. butter.
1 tsp. ginger.
1 pint flour.
1/2 cup sour milk.
1 tsp. soda.
1 egg.

Put the molasses and butter in a pan and set on the stove.

When the mixture boils up add the soda and ginger and take from the fire immediately.

Add the milk, the well-beaten egg and the flour, beat well.

Bake in a shallow cake pan in a rather quick oven for 20 minutes.

Lemon Sauce.

1 tbsp. cornstarch.
1/2 cup sugar.
1 pint boiling water.
1 tbsp. butter.
1 egg.
1 lemon.

Beat the egg, add the cornstarch and sugar, stir them well together; add the boiling water gradually and stir over the fire until thick; add the butter, juice and grated rind of one lemon.

Serve hot.

Vanilla Sauce.

1 cup milk.
2 (1.) tbsps. sugar. *
2 eggs.
1/2 tsp. vanilla.

Put the milk on to boil, beat the yolks and sugar till very light; add them to the boiling milk; stir over the fire until creamy. Have the whites beaten, pour over them the boiling mixture; beat thoroughly and serve at once.

* No explanation is offered for the "2 (1.) tbsps." above although earlier in her book, Adelaide Hoodless explains: "As there is such a diversity of opinion as to what constitutes a heaping spoonful, all the measurements given in this book will be by level spoonfuls."

CANADIAN WAR CAKE

Recipes for boiled raisin cakes made without eggs, butter, or milk, started appearing during the First World War and remained popular throughout the Great Depression and Second World War. Shortly after Canada joined the Second World War on September 10, 1939, the standby boiled raisin cake got a new patriotic name: Canada's War Cake or a variation of the same, such as Canadian War Cake.

Food quickly became a central part of Canada's war effort. The nation increased its food production capacity to help feed Britain, which was paramount after the fall of France in 1940, when Canadian food exports provided a lifeline to Britain. "Food will win the war," the catchphrase coined by Herbert Hoover, head of U.S. Food Administration during the First World War, became a popular Canadian slogan.

Mandatory Rations

By 1942, Canada had introduced mandatory food rationing. No one was exempt. Sugar, tea, coffee, butter, beer, wine, and spirits were rationed from 1942 until 1947. Meat was also rationed during 1943 and 1944. Rationing recipes became both popular and necessary.

This war cake recipe comes from the collection of Frances Mae (MacRae) Green (1928-1996). Frances was born in London, Ontario and was the great-great-great granddaughter of George T. Ward, founder of Wardsville, Upper Canada, which was incorporated in 1801. George T. Ward fought alongside Colonel George Talbot in the War of 1812.

The cake recipe came to Frances via her mother, Agnes Mae (Prout) MacRae (1888 – 1980), who was born in Bothwell, Ontario, and later lived in the nearby towns of London and Lambeth. Agnes worked as a seamstress who made her own patterns, and later took a job sorting vegetables on the assembly line, where she worked until she was 78 years old. She was a member of the Lambeth Garden Club, the United Church Women, and a euchre club. She was a wonderful grandmother who would make popcorn without the lid on the pan for the sheer joy of the flying popcorn and would play tiddly-winks with her grandchildren all Sunday afternoon. She was a tiny woman but there was nothing small about her personality: she could talk for hours.

Canada's War Cake

1 cup brown sugar
1 cup water
1 tbsp lard or shortening
½ tsp salt
1 ½ cups raisins
½ tsp each cinnamon and cloves

Boil all above together for 5 minutes and when cold, add 1½ cups of flour and ½ tsp baking soda. Bake in a greased cake pan at 325°F/165°C for about 40 minutes or until top springs back lightly when pressed.

UPSIDE-DOWN CAKES

Cake making changed drastically in the early 1920s, thanks to Ontario engineer and inventor Thomas Ahearn who in 1892 filed patent no. 39916 for the world's first "Electric Oven," a device Ahearn invented at Ottawa's Windsor Hotel.

The electric stove debuted at the 1893 Chicago World's Fair, but it was some years before the electric stove actually caught on, mostly because cities and towns were not yet connected to electricity grids. By the 1920s electric stoves were in use and by the 1930s they were becoming commonplace. And with the new technology came sweeping changes in baking – especially in bread and cake making.

All Manner of Cakes

Upside-down cakes first appeared in the late 1800s, usually made in a cast iron skillet, baked in a wood or coal fired cast iron stove. Temperatures were difficult to regulate and cake making required steady, specific temperatures.

When electric stoves replaced old stoves, cake making really took off. Pineapple Upside-Down Cakes, Apple Upside-Down Cakes (such as Tarte Tatin), and other cakes including chiffon, red velvet, and rich chocolate cakes, soon followed suit.

Ginger Pear Upside-Down Cake

3 tbsp butter
1 can pears
1 cup brown sugar
Blend butter and sugar, spread over bottom of greased cake pan, drain pears and arrange cut side up on sugar, butter mixture

Batter for cake:
½ cup butter
1 cup brown sugar
2 eggs, well-beaten
¾ cup molasses
2 ½ cups flour
2 tsp baking soda
1 tsp ground ginger
½ tsp salt
1 cup sour milk

Cream butter, add sugar, well-beaten eggs, molasses. Sift dry ingredients and add alternately with sour milk. Cover pears with this mixture and bake at 350° F (175°C) for 40 minutes or until cake is cooked and springs back when touched. Turn upside down and serve warm with whipped cream.

Ginger Pear Upside-Down Cake, from the Navy League I.O.D.E Victory Cook Book, 1941

NANA LANGFORD'S GUMDROP CAKE

Margaret (Doyle) Langford was born in Hamilton, Ontario in 1898. She married W.E. "Wilf" Langford, a First World War veteran who had served as an ambulance driver in Siberia during the war, before graduating from the Ontario College of Pharmacy in 1921.

The couple moved to Waterdown, where Wilf Langford set up his business in one half of the local grocery store. No sooner was the pharmacy set up when fire destroyed the building. The Langfords set to work, rebuilding their pharmacy – a business that lasted for another 64 years. Wilf, the son of a farmer, catered to the pharmaceutical needs of both animals and humans. In 1921, if the horses couldn't work, everything stopped.

Joan Langford circa 1938

Margaret was soon busy with four children, Mary Margaret, Kay, Joan, and Tom. As the children grew up they were frequent visitors to the pharmacy, which had the area's first and only counter service soda fountain complete with twirly chairs. The store including the soda fountain remained virtually unchanged until the doors closed for the last time in 1988.

A Serious Job

Joan (Langford) Lavery, the third of the Langford children, was born in 1935. On family trips to the Muskokas for Christmas, with the car packed to the rafters, Joan was entrusted with the important task of travelling with her mother's Gumdrop Cake on her lap and keeping the cake out of harm's way. A very serious job.

When Joan grew up and had a family of her own, she made this cake for her four children, who always knew it as "Nana Langford's Gumdrop cake."

Gumdrops have been around since the early 1800s. The cake came later, recipes for it were appearing by the early 1940s.

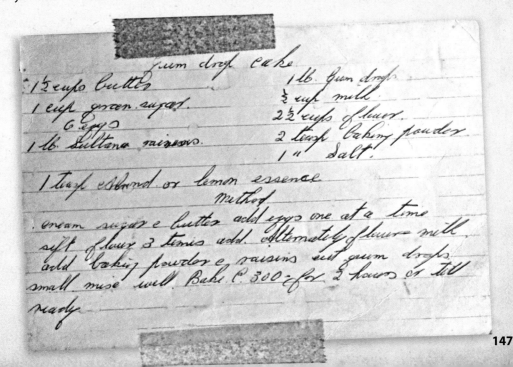

Nana Langford's Gumdrop Cake

1½ cups (12 oz or 340 g) butter
1 cup sugar
6 eggs
1 lb (454 g) sultana raisins)
1 lb (454 g) gum drops (no black ones, eat them while no one is looking)
½ cup milk
2 ½ cups flour
2 tsp baking powder
1 tsp salt
1 tbsp vanilla, almond, or lemon essence

Cream the sugar and butter and add the eggs one at a time. Sift the flour, salt, and baking powder and add alternately with the milk and essence. Add the raisins and gum drops. Mix well. Spoon into a well-greased bundt cake pan. Bake at 300°F (150°C) for about 1½ hours. Half the recipe will make a good-sized loaf, adjust the cooking time accordingly (about 40–45 minutes should do it.) This cake improves with age but should be wrapped and refrigerated if not eaten within a day or two of making.

(Right) Cowans Cake Icings advertisement From: the *Canadian Farm Cook Book,* 1911

When you want your cakes to look and taste a little extra fine use

Cowan's
Cake Icings

Besides getting the best results, you will save yourself a lot of work and bother. Cowan's Cake Icings are prepared ready for use—you can ice a cake in three minutes if you use them.

Chocolate, Pink, White, Lemon, Orange, Almond, Maple and Cocoanut Cream.

THE COWAN COMPANY LIMITED
TORONTO, ONTARIO

A CAKE FIT FOR A QUEEN

The origins of the Queen Elizabeth Cake are somewhat obscure. Some say it was served for the coronation of Queen Elizabeth II in 1953. Others believe it was invented for the 1937 coronation of King George VI and Queen Elizabeth, the Queen Mother.

A recipe in the *Opti-Mrs. Cook Book*, published in Kingston, Ontario, in 1950, three years before the coronation of Queen Elizabeth II, would tend to support the theory that the cake was invented for the Queen Mother.

Queen Elizabeth Cake

Adapted slightly from the *Opti-Mrs. Cook Book*, 1950, as submitted by Dorothy Phillips.

1 cup boiling water
1½ cups chopped cooking dates
½ tsp soda
¼ cup butter or shortening
1 cup white sugar
2 eggs, beaten
1 tsp vanilla
1 ½ cups flour
1 tsp baking powder
½ tsp salt
½ cup nuts

Pour boiling water over dates and baking soda and let stand until cool. Meanwhile, cream the sugar and butter. Add the beaten eggs and sifted dry ingredients. Add this mixture to the date mixture. Stir in the nuts. Bake in a greased 8x8 inch pan at 350 degrees for 30-35 minutes.

Topping:
6 tbsp brown sugar
½ cup coconut
2 tbsp butter
3-4 tbsp cream

Bring all the ingredients to the boil in a small saucepan over medium high heat. Boil gently for three minutes, stirring constantly. Spread over cake and place the cake under the broiler. Watch carefully and remove the first moment the topping begins to turn golden brown.

BUTTERNUT AND HICKORY NUT CAKES

Butternut trees (*Juglans cinerea*) are a member of the walnut family. They were once common throughout most of southern Ontario and sought after for both their fruit and wood. The nuts, sometimes called white walnuts, are said to have a number of powerful medicinal properties and were used by Indigenous Peoples to remedy a variety of conditions.

The trees are now on the endangered-species list due in large part to a fungal disease known as Butternut Canker, which has devastated the Butternut tree population. The trees like well-drained soil and tend to grow on the edge of forests and along stream banks. Known Butternut trees should be reported to the Ontario Ministry of Natural Resources to help with potential recovery strategies.

BUTTERNUT CAKE.—1 cup sugar, ½ cup butter, ½ cup sweet milk, ½ cup raisins, 1 cup butternut meats, 2 eggs, 2 cups flour, 2 teaspoons baking powder. Walnut meats can be used if preferred.—MRS. JAS. MABEE, Guysboro, Ont.

This recipe is from the *Canadian Farm Cook Book*

Shagbark Hickory trees (*Carya ovata*) are found along the St. Lawrence River, though stands of the trees have been found near Lake Huron and Georgian Bay, thought to have been planted hundreds of years ago by Indigenous Peoples. Shagbark Hickory trees can live for 200 years. The trees are identifiable by their rough, shaggy bark. The sweet nuts are a favourite of both humans and squirrels.

HICKORY-NUT CAKE

Miss Macallister, Kingston.

One cupful of shelled hickory nuts, one cupful of butter, one of sugar, one cupful of sifted flour, one-half cupful of corn starch, one-half cupful of milk, one and a-half teaspoonsful of baking powder, whites of four eggs, mix butter and sugar to a cream, add the whites, beaten lightly, milk, flour and lastly the nuts, first dredging them well in flour. Flavour to taste.

This Hickory Nut Cake recipe is from *The Canadian Economist*.

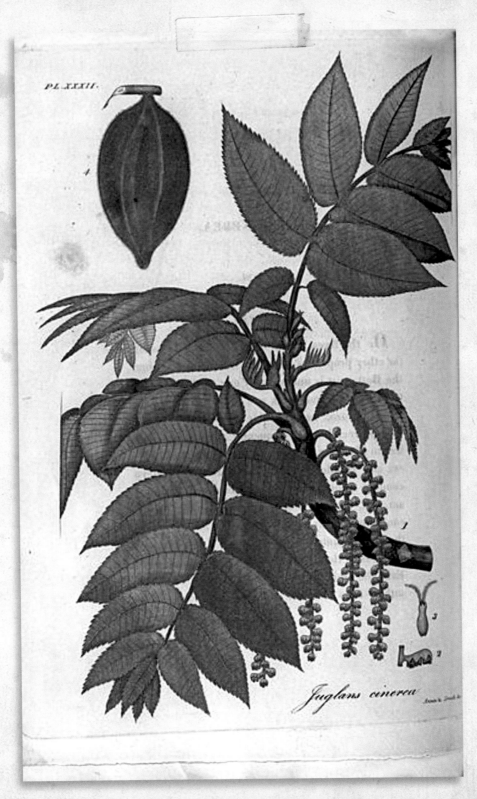

Butternut Tree (*Juglans cinerea*) Botanical Illustration Plate XXXII *American Medical Botany*, 1817

Mrs Merritt
Country-Club Luncheon
June 28th

Mrs Scott

BUTTER TARTS

Butter tarts are to Ontario what Nanaimo Bars are to British Columbia, Flapper Pie is to the Prairies, Tarte au Sucre to Quebec, and Figgy Duff is to Newfoundland: beloved and iconic. Essential pieces of our culinary history.

The original butter tart recipe is thought to be the one printed in the *Royal Victoria Cook Book*, a fundraiser compiled by the Women's Auxiliary of the Royal Victoria Hospital in Barrie, in 1900. The two-line recipe, shown below, entitled, "Filling for Tarts" submitted by Mrs. M. MacLeod, is the earliest known printed recipe for what we have fondly come to know as butter tarts.

PIES.

"Who'll dare deny the truth, there's poetry in pies."—*Longfellow.*

PUFF PASTE.—One pound of flour, ½ pound lard, ½ pound of butter. Mix flour and lard together, wet with a little cold or ice water, flatten out on board and spread with some of the butter, roll up and flatten out again. Repeat, adding the butter in this way until all the butter is rolled in. Set on ice until thoroughly chilled.

Mrs. C. J. McRae, Stayner.

PLAIN PIE CRUST.—Sift a level teaspoon of baking powder with a coffee cup of flour and a pinch of salt. Into this chop with a knife 2 tablespoons lard, working thoroughly and quickly, then stir in ¼ cup of ice-cold water. Set the dough on ice to chill and use this quantity for 1 pie.

Miss L. McCarthy.

FILLING FOR TARTS.—One cup sugar, ½ cup butter, 2 eggs, 1 cup currants; mix. Fill the tarts and bake.

Mrs. Malcolm MacLeod.

CHOCOLATE PIE.—One and three-quarter cups of sweet milk, 3 tablespoons of grated chocolate, 2 eggs, 1 cup of sugar, vanilla. Put the milk and chocolate over the fire to dissolve the chocolate. Beat the yolks of the eggs, sugar and vanilla together and add to the milk. Bake with an under crust When cooked beat the whites to a stiff froth, add a little sugar and heap on the pie. Return to the oven and color a slight brown. Mrs. H. B. Myers.

MINCE MEAT.—One pound almonds chopped up, 1 pound raisins, 1 pound currants, 1 pound suet, 1 pound apples chopped up fine, ½ pound sugar, ¼ pound candied

THE BEANERY QUEEN'S BUTTER TARTS

Shirley Jack began her career as a beanery queen in the Canadian National Railway's Rainy River station, before moving on to other northern CNR stations in Armstrong and Nakina. Beanery was railroad slang for a railway eating house and beanery queens were waitresses.

Railways were once all important in Canada, opening up the North and connecting the vast country long before highways served the purpose. Railway communities sprang up around stations, where workers were needed for services like restaurants, one of the few job opportunities available to young females – many of whom arrived looking only to gain work experience but ended up staying. In Shirley's case, her move to Nakina lasted 60 years.

From Waitress to Cook

Shirley Jack's parents were farmers in Manitoba, though her heritage included emigrants to Ontario, American Planters, British Loyalists, Germans, and an Irish-South Asian grandmother. Shirley learned to cook young, a skill that stood her in good stead as she went from being a waitress to a cook, and it helped too when she married Bruno Kouhi and soon had seven children to feed.

The baking skills she developed on the family farm and then honed in the beanery kitchens also helped to supplement the family income. Years after Shirley Jack worked in the beanery kitchens, her customers still remembered her and her legendary butter tarts.

Shirley Jack's Butter Tarts (recipe supplied by Beverly Soloway)

½ cup raisins, soaked in boiling water for about 10 minutes, then drained
¼ cup melted butter
½ cup brown sugar
¼ tsp salt
½ cup corn syrup
1 egg, slightly beaten
1 tsp vanilla

Pastry
1 ½ cups flour
2 tbsp white sugar
1/3 tsp salt
½ tsp baking powder
½ cup lard
Cold water

In mixing bowl, combine raisins, melted butter, brown sugar, salt, and corn syrup. Mix well. Add egg and vanilla. Mix. Put filling in refrigerator wile you make the pastry and prepare the tart shells. This can be done several hours in advance but be sure to stir the filling again before filling the shells.

For the pastry, mix the flour, white sugar, salt, and baking powder. Cut in the lard with a butter knife until mixture is crumbly. Sprinkle with cold water, handling as little as possible to make a ball of pastry. Roll out onto a floured board and cut 12 circles large enough to line muffins tins with pastry. Fill shells about 3/4 full. Bake at 400°F (205°C) for about 15 minutes maximum. Fill should still be bubbling and not completely set. Set on a wire rack to cool.

MATRIMONIAL SQUARES

Nobody seems to know for certain why these layered oatmeal-and-date squares are sometimes known as matrimonial squares. One theory is that the alternating layers of crumbly oatmeal and smooth date filling symbolize relationships: sometimes smooth and sweet, and sometimes crumbly and slightly rough-going. Or perhaps the name originated from the squares being served so often at matrimonial events.

In my household, they've only ever been known as oatmeal-date squares. Plain and simple.

Earliest Date Squares

The first recipes for date squares began appearing in the early 1900s. A recipe for Oatmeal Cookies filled with a cooked-date filling and a similar recipe for Date Cookies with a layer of cooked-date filling sandwiched between oatmeal layers both appeared in the 1909 cookbook, *Culinary Landmarks Sault Ste Marie*.

Most oatmeal-date square recipes are just versions of the same thing – all of them stemming from the old recipes. This is my own version, adapted from a vintage newspaper clipping.

Oatmeal Date Squares

Date Filling
1 lb (454 grams) pitted cooking dates
½ cup sugar
1 cup water
½ tsp salt
½ tbsp white vinegar
Bring the dates, ½ cup sugar, ¼ tsp salt, and vinegar to a boil. Turn the heat right down and cook for about 10-15 minutes or until dates are soft and mixture is jammy. Add a little more water if necessary. Allow to cool while preparing the oatmeal mixture.

Oatmeal base and top
1 cup brown sugar
2 cup quick cooking rolled oats
1 ½ cups all-purpose flour
½ tsp salt
1 cup salted butter, softened

Mix together the dry ingredients and cut in the butter until well mixed and crumbly. Firmly press just over half the oatmeal mixture into a buttered 9 x13 x2 inch (33 x 23 x 5 cm) glass baking pan. Spread with the date filling. Sprinkle the remaining oatmeal mixture loosely over the filling.

Bake at 350°F [175°C] for 20-25 minutes. Let cool before cutting into squares.

MORE MATRIMONIAL BLISS

When the Second World War ended and rationing was finally lifted, home baking took off with a vengeance. Between the widespread use of newfangled electric ovens and brand-new ingredients like chocolate chips (introduced in 1941), as well as old standbys like sweetened condensed milk (introduced in 1856) – cookbooks in the 40s and early 50s were full of sweet treats with names like Heavenly Bars, Magic Squares, Honeymoon Squares, and Matrimonial Bliss.

The new recipes were not just sweet, but colourful too. During the Great Depression, Texan John A. Adams had built an empire selling vanilla essence and food colouring, such as that used in Red Velvet Cake.

This Matrimonial Cake has a thin shortbread base, followed with a sinfully delicious layer of brown sugar, walnut, cherry goodness (some similar recipes also included coconut); and is crowned with butter icing. The butter icing on these squares was often tinted pink. Perfect for wedding showers but irresistible no matter what the occasion. This version comes from the recipe collection of Joan (Langford) Lavery – whose mother's Gumdrop Cake is included earlier.

Matrimonial Cake

2 tsp gran sugar
1 cup flour
½ c butter

Mix together & spread in
8" pan (short bread)
Bake for 20 min - 325

then mix
1½ c brown sugar
2 tbsp flour
2 eggs
½ c red cherries
½ " walnuts

Spread on cake & put back
in oven & bake 20-25 min
Cool - Make a butter
icing & spread over
cake - Cut in squares

Matrimonial Cake (also known as Walnut Cherry Bars)

2 tsp sugar
1 cup flour
½ cup butter
Mix together and spread in a buttered 8-inch square pan. Bake for 20 minutes at 325°F. [Other recipes say to bake for 10 minutes - it will be baked again shortly....]

Then mix:
1 1/3 cup brown sugar
2 tbsp flour
2 eggs
½ cup red cherries (glace or maraschino)
½ cup chopped walnuts
[½ cup shredded coconut]
Spread on the shortbread base and put back in the oven for another 20-25 minutes. Cool. Make a butter icing [which can be tinted pink with maraschino cherry juice or red food colouring, if desired] and spread over cake. Cut in [small] squares.

Hotpoint Stove advertisement, 1923

120   Lord Salisbury Chapter, I.O.D.E. COOK BOOK

Hotpoint
The Name That Means
Correct Electric Cookery

PERFECT cooking has ceased to depend on long experience, and constant watchfulness over a hot range. With the Hotpoint Electric Range you can cook an entire meal and not even become flushed.

COOKING BY ELECTRICITY IS ECONOMICAL

The thick-walled, oven of a Hotpoint Range, retains every particle of heat and does not permit evaporation. This allows you to reduce the current, after cooking has commenced, and to finish on stored heat. You can duplicate any given temperature day after day invariably.

"Made in Canada" by

HOTPOINT DIVISION
of
Canadian General Electric Co., Limited

MY MOTHER'S GLAZED GINGER SHORTBREAD

This is one of the recipes my mother brought with her from England. It was one of her childhood favourites and it became one of mine too. I remember the days when I came home from school to find a pan of glazed ginger shortbread waiting on the counter for our afternoon snack.

I especially liked it when she made it in a round tin pie plate and cut the shortbread in pie-shaped wedges, called petticoat tails. Coming home to this shortbread and a cup of tea are still high on my list of childhood memories.

Shortbread has been made for centuries throughout Scotland and England but the first known printed recipe dates back to 1736. Shortbread typically follows a standard recipe of one-part sugar, two parts butter, three parts flour. Technically if there are additions, such as there are in my mother's recipe, it's no longer shortbread, but rather, shortcake. In honour of my mother, I'm sticking with calling this shortbread.

Glazed Ginger Shortbread

For the shortbread
½ cup (120 grams) butter, room temperature or slightly softened
½ cup sugar
1 ½ cups flour
1 tsp baking powder
1 tbsp ground ginger
Pinch of salt

Using a hand-held electric beater, mix together the butter and sugar. Add the flour, baking powder, ginger, and salt and mix until crumbly. Press the mixture into a lightly buttered 8-x 8- inch pan or as my mother used, an 8-inch tin pie plate. (I use a glass pie plate.) Bake at 325°F (165°C) for about 18 minutes or until golden (not browned). Remove from the oven and set to cool.

For the glaze
2 tbsp butter, melted
1 tbsp Lyle's Golden Syrup (corn syrup will do in an emergency)
2/3 cup icing sugar
2 tsp ground ginger
Pinch of salt

Melt together the butter and Lyle's Golden Syrup on the stove, or in the microwave. Add the icing sugar, ginger, and pinch of salt. Stir until mixed. Spread over slightly cooled shortbread. Cut in thin wedges (or bars if you used a square pan). Store in an airtight tin.

EMMA FAULK'S GINGER COOKIES

Emma's Ginger Cookies

2 cups white
sugar
1 cup brown sugar
1 ½ cups lard
3 eggs
3/4 cup cold coffee
1 pint molasses

2 tsp soda
3 tsp ground
ginger
1 tsp cloves
Salt
Flour

Mix all the ingredients and add enough flour to make a soft but roll-able dough. Roll dough lightly on a floured board and cut (with a Mason jar or large round cookie cutter). Place on greased baking sheets and bake at 350°F (175°C) until done (about 15 minutes). Remove from oven to wire racks and sprinkle with white sugar.

Norma (Erb) Cardiff (born in 1937) remembers, when she was just a little girl, going with her brother Jimmy to visit the 100-acre farm next door, where grownup brother and sister Emma and Johnny Faulk lived and worked. It was always an excitement to visit the big working farm, even though Norma and Jimmy lived on a farm themselves, albeit much smaller.

The side by side farms were on Pork Street, near Sebastopol in Perth County, Ontario, between Tavistock and Stratford. Neither of the properties had electricity. Both used wood burning stoves to cook and heat, and coal-oil lamps for lighting.

At times, when there were too many lambs for the mother sheep to feed, Norma and Jimmy were allowed to bottle feed the baby lambs in the Faulk's kitchen. And sometimes, Emma Faulk would make cookies – her ginger cookies were everyone's favourite.

Roll and Repeat

Emma would don a starched white apron that reached from just below her chin to just above her ankles and mix the ingredients in a large crock bowl on her kitchen table. Then she would cover the long, wide pine harvest table with white flour and begin to roll the dough from the table, right up onto her apron all the way up to and over her ample bosom in one seamless motion, and then all the way back down again, and repeat until the dough was perfectly rolled and just the right thickness.

With the dough laid across the table, Emma would take the heavy Mason jar that functioned as a cookie cutter and cut perfect circles. When the cookies were baked and removed from the old wood stove, Emma would sprinkle them with white sugar and set them to cool in front of the only window in the dark back kitchen while Norma and Jimmy waited eagerly for a taste.

EMPIRE BISCUITS

Empire Biscuits.

1/2 lb. Butter
1/2 cup fruit sugar
2 cups flour

1 egg.

Mix butter and sugar to a cream. Work in flour and then add egg unbeaten. Roll out and cut with cookie cutter. Bake in a slow oven for 10 min. to a golden brown. Ice with confectioners sugar and put to-gether in pairs with cherry or nut on top.

Empire Biscuits were popular throughout the United Kingdom and Commonwealth countries including Canada and New Zealand. In 1913, the British Empire included one quarter of the Earth's total land area and 23 percent of its population.

The biscuits were originally known as Linzer Cookies but with the outbreak of the First Wolrd War, the name was changed to Empire Biscuits. That name stuck even though the British Empire did not.

The final transfer of Hong Kong back to China in 1997 marked the final end of the British Empire.

This recipe comes from the collection of Bertha White, whose Golden Corn Cake recipe appears earlier. Her instructions say, "Ice with confectioners' sugar and put together in pairs …" Empire biscuits are typically made with two shortbread-like biscuits, sandwiched together with jam (usually raspberry), and finished with plain white icing (made of icing sugar and a little water), topped with a cherry or walnut.

ICE BOX COOKIES

Iceboxes date back the mid-1800s and by the end of the 19th century were a mainstay in most Ontario kitchens. They were often handsome pieces of furniture, made from wood, and lined with zinc and insulating materials to help keep the ice solid. Spigots or drip trays collected melting ice which was then used for cooking.

Ice Haulers in Ontario in the 1890s

Those who had access cut ice from frozen ponds, lakes, and rivers. The ice was stored in ice houses. The massive ice blocks, covered in sawdust, stayed frozen for surprisingly long periods. Those who didn't have access, or who didn't have an ice house, relied on ice haulers for deliveries.

As cities grew, ice became contaminated with industrial and sewage runoff. When early refrigeration technology became available, ice factories began producing ice from safer municipal water supplies for home delivery. Eventually that technology was replaced with home refrigerators, although Canadians were surprisingly slow adopting the change from iceboxes to home refrigerators.

In 1941, a mere 20.9 percent of Canadian households had a refrigerator. By 1951, nearly 50 percent of households had made the change. By 1967, an estimated 97.2 percent of households had a refrigerator,[39] and Ice Box cookies had been renamed Refrigerator Cookies.

Ice Box Christmas Cookies

1 cup soft butter
3/4 cup brown sugar
½ tsp vanilla
1/8 tsp salt
2 ½ cups sifted Purity Flour
1 cup almonds, sliced lengthwise
½ cup each red and green glace cherries, whole

Cream butter, add sugar and then add vanilla, salt, and flour.

Finally add nuts and cherries and form into rolls. Leave in ice box overnight. Slice thinly with a sharp knife and bake on greased baking sheets in moderate oven (350°F) for 10 minutes.

Ice Box Christmas Cookies from the Purity Cook Book, 1945

POPCORN BALLS

Popcorn is one of the six major types of corn: dent corn, flint corn, pod corn, popcorn, flour corn, and sweet corn. According to evidence found in Mexico, popcorn has been eaten by Indigenous Peoples for thousands of years.

Here in Canada, Father Joseph Francois Lafitau, who spent six years in New France (now Quebec) beginning in 1711, saw corn being used to make popcorn by Indigenous people. Lafitau described a type of maize which the Iroquois called orgarita that when exposed to heat burst forth like a flower. Father Lafitau found this to be a superior use for maize and noted that it was especially liked by the French.[40]

One of the first known recipes for Popcorn Balls came from the 1861 American cookbook, the *Housekeeper's Encyclopedia*, by E.F. Haskell: "Boil honey, maple, or other sugar to the great thread; pop corn and stick the corn together in balls with the candy."

Popcorn Balls

1 ¼ cups sugar
1 ¼ cups light brown sugar
½ cup light corn syrup
2/3 cup water
1 tbsp butter
3 ½ quarts popped corn
1 ¼ tsp salt

Put the sugar, brown sugar, corn syrup, and water in a saucepan [over medium-high heat], stirring until the sugar is dissolved.

Add the butter and continue cooking, without stirring, until the temperature 240°F is reached, or until it forms soft ball when tested in cold water. Put popped corn in a large bowl and sprinkle with salt. Pour hot syrup over it and mix thoroughly.

Form in small balls. Wrap in wax paper.

Popcorn Balls from *The Alexandra Club Cook Book*

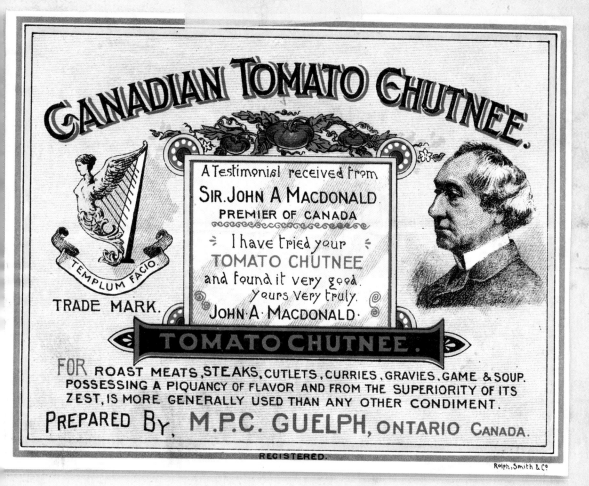

THE INTRODUCTION OF HOME CANNING

Before Mason jars were invented by American John Mason in 1858, the preservation of food was considerably more difficult.

The precursor to Mason jars was a method of airtight food preservation using glass jars and wax sealers – a process invented by French chef and confectioner Nicolas Appert, who is known as the "father of canning."

Lime and Cheese

Appert experimented with many methods of canning, including using champagne bottles and a sealing compound of lime and cheese. Luckily, he lived to keep experimenting. By 1803 he was using wide-mouth jars and wax sealants and his foods were being used by the French military.

In 1810, Appert was awarded a twelve-thousand-franc prize by French Emperor Napoléon Bonaparte, who had offered the prize to anyone who could design a safe, new method to preserve food. Appert's method was to place food in thick, largemouth glass jars sealed with wax sealers, then submerse the jars in boiling water until the food was appropriately cooked. The process became known as "Appertization."

It would be fair to say that between them, Appert and Mason successfully revolutionized food storage, particularly for home canners, who using the technology were able to safely preserve all manner of foods including fruits and vegetables – a particular boon for those who had to endure long winters and late springs with little access to anything other than salted meat, game, fish, and bread for months on end.

Family Jars

Jars of jelly, jars of jam,
Jars of potted beef and ham.
Jars of early gooseberries nice,
Jars of mincemeat, jars of spice,
Jars of orange marmalade,
Jars of pickles, all home-made,
Jars of cordial elder wine,
Jars of honey superfine.
Would the only jars were these,
Which occur in families.

From the *Canadian Agriculturalist*, April 1855, Author unknown.

CHESTNUT JAM

WINTER JAMS.

CHESTNUT JAM.

Boil the chestnuts in water, and when tender, peel them. Pass through a fine sieve and weigh the puree, allowing an equal weight of finely powdered sugar. Flavor with vanilla and put all in a preserving pan. Cook gently for 45 minutes, stirring well all the time. Place in pots and cover when cool.

Though chestnuts are native to the temperate regions of the Northern Hemisphere, the American chestnut tree (*Castanea dentata*), which produces edible chestnuts, is on the endangered list due to a fungal disease. The only known surviving American chestnut trees in Canada are all in southwestern Ontario. Known American chestnut trees should be reported to the Ontario Ministry of Natural Resources to help with potential recovery strategies.

Conkers

If you're picking chestnuts in Ontario be warned that horse chestnuts (also known as conkers) from the horse-chestnut tree (*Aesculus hippocastanum*) are poisonous and should not be eaten.

Most chestnuts sold in Canada come from either Europe or Asia. Chestnuts can be used in a variety of ways but must be cooked before eating. They are excellent in desserts, stuffing, or served roasted as an appetizer. This chestnut-jam recipe, from an old newspaper clipping found tucked in a very old cookbook, would be wonderful sandwiched between layers of meringue; stirred into plain yogurt; folded into whipped cream and served with poached pears; or spread on buttered toast.

Please note: Because many of the following recipes do not include instructions for proper sealing, all should be sealed while hot in sterilized jars and processed using the boiling water bath technique.

GINGERED PEAR CONSERVE

Pare and core eight pounds of hard pears and run through the mincer with three lemons from which the seeds have been removed. Chop fine half a pound or more of preserved ginger. Put all into a preserving kettle with six pounds of sugar and four cloves. Cook slowly for several hours till the fruit is clear and the syrup rich. Seal hot.

Gingered Pear Conserve from *The Family Herald Cook Book*, 1924

CRABAPPLE JELLY

Cut up clean, washed crab apples into quarters, without peeling; add half as much water and cook till the apples are soft. Strain the juice through cheesecloth as long as it will drip, then strain it again through a flannel bag. To every quart of juice add a quart of granulated sugar. Stir over the fire until the sugar is dissolved. Bring to the boiling point, skim; boil again, skim; and repeat a third time. Use sterilized glasses into which to pour the hot liquid.

Crab-apple Jelly from *The Family Herald Cook Book*, 1924

RHUBARB-ALMOND MARMALADE

Four pounds of rhubarb, washed and cut; four pounds of sugar, four lemons, the grated yellow rind of one lemon; small quantity of almonds (sweet) blanched and shredded. Mix all and let stand over night then cook slowly until done. Seal hot in small jars.

Rhubarb Almond Marmalade from *The Family Herald Cook Book*, 1924

CRANBERRY MARMALADE.

—1 quart cranberries, 1 pint water, boil together until cooked; then add 1 pound white sugar, ½ pound raisins, 10 cents' worth chopped walnuts, grated rind and juice of 2 oranges. Boil this 20 minutes.—Mrs. C. O. Bennett, Clearmont, Ont.

Cranberry Marmalade from the *Canadian Farm Cook Book*, 1911
N.B. For the "10 cents' worth of walnuts," try substituting ½ cup finely chopped walnuts.

SWEET INDIAN CHUTNEY
Mrs. W. F. Willoughby.

3 pounds sugar
2 ounces salt
½ pound mustard seed
½ pound raisins
¼ pound ginger root (in bag)

½ pound onions
⅛ ounce cayenne
1 quart vinegar
10 sour apples
5 ripe tomatoes (large)

Chop apples, onions, raisins, tomatoes, before putting on to boil with other ingredients. Boil all slowly for 5 hours and seal while hot.

MUSTARD PICKLE
Mrs. R. B. Rice.

2 quarts small gherkins
1 cauliflower
2 quarts small cucumbers.

2 quarts small onions
1 head of celery

Cut cauliflower, celery and cucumbers into small sections. Put all in brine for 24 hours. Scald in same and drain.

Paste:—8 tablespoons best mustard
2 tablespoons turmeric
3 quarts cider vinegar

2 cups granulated sugar
1 cup flour

Mix flour, sugar, mustard and turmeric together with cold vinegar. Put remainder on to boil. When boiling remove from the fire and add the paste. When well mixed return to fire and boil well. Pour over pickles while hot.

Crab Apple Catsup.

Three pounds crab apples, one and a third pounds sugar, boil until thick, one pint vinegar, one tablespoonful ground cloves, one tablespoonful black pepper, one teaspoonful salt.

(Top) Sweet Indian Chutney from *The Wimodausis Club Cook Book, Toronto*, 1922

(Middle) Mustard Pickle from *The Wimodausis Club Cook Book*, Toronto, 1922

(Bottom) Crab Apple Catsup from *The New Galt Cook Book*, 1898

Grandmother Cronk's Pickled Pears 1830

12 lbs pears
4 lbs sugar
1-quart vinegar
Cloves

Bring the sugar, vinegar, and cloves to a boil in a large pan.

Add the whole peeled pears (stems and core in tact). Cook until the pears are tender, about 20 minutes and the sugar syrup is thickened. Bottle in sterilized jars. [Use the boiling water bath method to ensure safe processing.] Will keep for six months without refrigeration.

Grandmother Cronk's Pickled Pears 1830 from the Museums of Prince Edward County

Brandied Peaches* from *The Boston Cooking-School Cook Book*, 1911
 *Note that this recipe can easily be scaled to suit. 1 peck of peaches = 12 pounds or 5.4 kg.
One quart = 4 cups, or just under a litre.

Brandied Peaches

1 peck peaches   Half their weight in sugar
              1 quart high-proof alcohol or brandy

Remove skins from peaches, and put alternate layers of peaches and sugar in a stone jar; then add alcohol. Cover closely, having a heavy piece of cloth under cover of jar.

THE MUCH-OVERLOOKED WALNUT

Walnuts from Ontario's many black walnut trees (*Juglans regia*) may just be our greatest missed foraging opportunity. The black walnut tree was once revered for both its wood and its fruit but has fallen into disfavour because the trees release a chemical called juglone into the surrounding soil, which causes toxic reactions to some plants growing in the vicinity. The walnut fruit itself is not toxic.

The nut kernels were popular with Indigenous Peoples and early settlers who lived within the range of the tree. There are reports of settlers storing large sacks of walnuts each year and early cookbooks included recipes for walnuts used in many dishes, including salads, soups, cakes, stuffing, jams, relishes, and walnut ketchup.

A Delicacy
The early fruit before the nut shell develops can be pickled and is considered a delicacy. The nuts can also be eaten, dried, and shelled. In the southern United States, black walnuts are still harvested commercially, and millions of pounds of black walnuts are sold domestically.

Pickled walnuts, often paired with Stilton cheese, or served as part of a ploughman's lunch, have been a delicacy in England since at least the early 1700s. They are a perfect addition to a charcuterie platter.

PICKLED WALNUTS

Many persons do not enjoy pickled walnuts because they consider them too salt and too highly spiced. In fact, salt and spice are often all that can be tasted when eating pickled walnuts. The following recipe from the stillroom of an old English manor house preserves the nutty flavor and ensures against over salting. Choose a hundred young and rather small walnuts. Do not prick them. Lay them is strong salt and water for eight days, changing the brine once. Then lay the nuts in the sun—they will soon blacken. Boil in a cup of vinegar for ten minutes, four teaspoonfuls of whole black pepper, eight allspice, and four cloves, and allow to cool. Pack the walnuts into jars, and divide the boiled vinegar and spices between the jars. Fill up with cold malt vinegar, which, if desired, may have been boiled previously. They will be ready in three months, and will be found delicious.

Pickled Walnuts* from *The Family Herald Cook Book*, 1924

*A note about pickling walnuts – the immature green fruits must be gathered early in the season, before the shells start to form. A recipe from an old English cookbook advises that you should be able to pierce the skin with a regular dressmaker's pin, in order to test the suitability of the walnuts for pickling. Also, a cup of brown sugar added to the vinegar and spice solution above augments the flavour.

RUTH REDMOND'S VEGETABLE MARROW CHUTNEY

References to "vegetable marrows" appear in many early cookbooks and recipe collections. They are popular in Britain, where giant marrows are grown competitively, much like pumpkins are in North America. The vegetable marrow is merely the mature fruit of a certain Cucurbita pepo cultivar (which includes pattypan squash, yellow summer squash, zucchini, and pumpkins). The immature fruit of the same cultivar is known as zucchini in North America.

Vegetable marrows were often served stuffed as a main course in Great Britain and also in Canada. Recipes for fried, boiled, stuffed, and stewed vegetable marrow, as well as vegetable-marrow rissoles and vegetable-marrow chutney, appeared in early Canadian cookbooks.

Vegetable Marrow Chutney

12 cups (4 lbs) vegetable marrow measured after peeling, seeding, and dicing
8 cups sugar, brown or white
½ oz (about 30) tiny red dried chili peppers, finely crumbled
20 garlic cloves, peeled, and finely chopped
1 oz bruised ginger root or 3 tsp powdered ginger
1 cup seedless raisins
2 tbsp salt
1 cup cider vinegar

In a large, heavy kettle, combine vegetable marrow and sugar (no water) and cook over medium heat, stirring frequently until marrow is clear, approximately 50 minutes.

Add remaining ingredients and bring to boil. Keep at steady boil until desired consistency is achieved, approximately an hour (should be soft jam-like consistency but not solid as it will thicken more upon cooling).

Pour into sterile jars and seal immediately. When sealed properly, will store in cool dark place for approximately six months. Can also be sealed with wax or given a hot water bath for safe storage.

This recipe from the collection of Ruth Redmond, whose carrot soufflé recipe appears earlier, calls for 12 cups or 4 pounds of vegetable marrow. Overgrown zucchini would work perfectly.

FAVOURITE BREAD AND BUTTER PICKLES

Bread and butter pickles are a longstanding favourite in Canadian kitchens. The recipe was said to have been invented in Illinois, by Omar and Cora Fanning, who filed and received a patent for their trademark sweet-and-sour Fannings Bread and Butter Pickles in 1923. The name stems from the fact that the Fannings, a farm couple struggling to make ends meet, apparently traded their pickles with local shop owners for staples such as bread and butter.

Curiously, plenty of recipes for sweet-and-sour cucumber pickles pre-date the Fanning's recipe, including one in *The New Galt Cook Book*, published in Toronto in 1898. The recipe, entitled simply, "Ripe Cucumber Pickle" calls for, among other things, cucumbers, salt, one-quart of white vinegar, one pound of white sugar, and cassia (similar to cinnamon).

My university roommate, Joanne Lavery, used to bring several jars of her mother's Bread and Butter Pickles to campus with her. They were, and still are, my favourite pickles. The recipe, passed down in her family, found its way to me, and I've made them ever since. The trick to these pickles is slicing the cucumbers incredibly thinly.

Bread and Butter Pickles

30 cups wafer thin cucumber slices (use small cucumbers)
8 small white onions, very finely sliced
½ cup pickling (coarse) salt
4 trays of ice cubes
5 cups white vinegar
5 cups sugar
2 tsp mustard seeds
1 tsp turmeric
1 tsp celery seeds * don't skip these!

Sterilize canning jars.
Wash cucumbers and slice very finely. Your food processor may not slice thinly enough – you want these slices to be almost transparent. I use a very sharp knife and a cutting board and plenty of patience. A mandolin would also work well.

Slice onion finely and separate rings. Place the sliced cucumbers and onion in a large bowl and cover with salt and ice. Let stand overnight in a cool place.

In the morning, drain thoroughly but don't rinse. Mix all remaining ingredients in a large canning kettle and bring to the boil. Simmer for 5 minutes. Add the drained cucumbers and onions and return the pot to the boil. Remove from heat and can immediately.

186   *Lord Salisbury Chapter, I.O.D.E., COOK BOOK*

"Health is the first good lent to man,"
—HERRICK

The Natural Health Drink

ENO is just a sparkling pleasant health drink that in a perfectly natural manner stimulates sluggish organs, clears away injurious residues, and invigorates and fortifies the entire system. Throughout the world for half a century Eno has been acknowledged the standard restorative for digestive ailments. *Take just a dash of Eno in a glass of water every morning on rising.*

ENO's "FRUIT SALT"
TRADE MARK

Prepared only by
J. C. Eno, Ltd.
London, Eng.

Sales Representative for North America
Harold F. Ritchie & Co., Ltd.
10-18 McCaul St. Toronto.

M-3

TRADTIONAL INDIGENOUS DRINKS

Berry Drink

This is a traditional First Nations beverage made with seasonal, regional berries. It is simple, refreshing, and surprisingly delicious and
can be made easily in whatever quantity is required.

1 cup or 250 ml cold water
¼ - ½ cup fresh seasonal berries (blueberries, raspberries,
blackberries, strawberries, or other regional fresh berries) mashed
1 tbsp maple syrup

Stir together and keep chilled until serving time. Can be made by
the pitcher, just adjust ingredients accordingly.

Cedar Tea

This traditional drink among some Indigenous Peoples, is notably high
in Vitamin C. It was introduced to the first Europeans in order to
help them avoid scurvy, especially in winter. In small quantities it
has a number of beneficial qualities. In large quantities, cedar tea is
toxic. Cedar is sacred to many Indigenous Peoples and a thanksgiving
is offered when harvesting boughs from the trees. Take only as
much cedar as you will use.

2-3 cups freshly picked cedar bough tips
water
maple syrup to sweeten
½ tsp cinnamon or a cinnamon stick

Wash the cedar boughs and drain. Place in a large pot and cover
with water. Bring to the boil and then drain the water - this is to
help eliminate toxins. Replace the water with 6 cups of fresh water
and add the cinnamon and bring to a boil again, for about 5-10
minutes or until the water takes on a tea-like colour. Strain the tea
and serve hot or cold. Add maple syrup to taste.

THE REINVENTION OF SHRUB

Shrub is an old-fashioned, fermented, fruity drink made two different ways. The first method involves making a fruit, sugar, and vinegar syrup (as in the Raspberry Shrub recipe below). Water or carbonated water (and optionally, alcohol) are added to serve.

Contemporary recipes for shrub made this way typically call for about five cups of ripe fruit and their weight in sugar, left to sit for 24 hours before straining and then adding to the strained liquid an equal measure of vinegar. The recipe below adds the vinegar first and the sugar later.

A Second Method
The second method of making shrub is to mix alcohol (traditionally brandy, whisky, or rum are used, although vodka is a contemporary favourite) with fruit and sugar. Once the mixture has steeped, it can be strained and served diluted with water or soda water.

Shrub can be made of many fresh ripe fruits including strawberries, blueberries, blackberries, cherries, plums, peaches, apricots, cranberries, and even rhubarb. Some combinations such as black cherries and white vinegar mixed with balsamic, or peach and white wine vinegar work particularly well. Raspberry shrub is a classic.

Raspberry Shrub

4 quarts red raspberries
1-quart white vinegar
White sugar

Pour vinegar over berries and let stand four days.

Strain.

To each pint of juice add 1 pound of white sugar. Boil 20 minutes, bottle and keep in a cool place.

To use, dilute with ice water [or soda water]. Refreshing on hot days.

Raspberry Shrub from the *Opti-Mrs. Cook Book*, 1950.

Choice small fruit – perfect for shrub - from the Henry G. Gilbert Nursery and Seed Catalog, 1904

MRS. BEETON MAKES COCKTAILS

Mrs. Beeton included an extensive collection of recipes for homemade wines, liqueurs, and cocktails in her *Book of Household Management*, later to be renamed *Mrs. Beeton's Cookery Book*. Amongst the wine recipes are elderberry, ginger, cowslip, gooseberry and rhubarb; as well as drinking vinegar (also known as shrub) and mead (honey wine).

In addition, Mrs. Beeton included recipes for homemade beer, liqueurs, and a selection of cocktails including several "Cup" recipes, like the Claret Cup and Champagne Cup cocktail recipes below, served in a large communal silver cup. By 1906, she had adjusted the recipes so that they were no longer served in communal bowls, and added a note to the Champagne Cup recipe to say, "Seasonable in summer or for a dance at any time."

Claret Cup

1831. INGREDIENTS. —1 bottle of claret, 1 bottle of soda-water, about 1/2 lb. of pounded ice, 4 tablespoonfuls of powdered sugar, 1/4 teaspoonful of grated nutmeg, 1 liqueur-glass of Maraschino, a sprig of green borage.*

Mode.—Put all the ingredients into a silver cup, regulating the proportion of ice by the state of the weather: if very warm, a larger quantity would be necessary. Hand the cup round with a clean napkin passed through one of the handles, that the edge of the cup may be wiped after each guest has partaken of the contents thereof.

Champagne-Cup

1832. INGREDIENTS. — 1-quart bottle of champagne, 2 bottles of soda-water, 1 liqueur-glass of brandy or Curaçoa, 2 tablespoonfuls of powdered sugar, 1 lb. of pounded ice, a sprig of green borage. *

Mode. — Put all the ingredients into a silver cup; stir them together and serve the same as claret-cup No. 1831. Should the above proportion of sugar not be found sufficient to suit some tastes, increase the quantity. When borage is not easily obtainable, substitute for it a few slices of cucumber-rind.
Seasonable. — Suitable for picnics, balls, weddings, and other festive occasions.

Claret Cup and Champagne-Cup from *Mrs. Beeton's Book of Household Management*, 1861

*Borage (Borago officinalis) is an annual flowering herb that was traditionally used for its medicinal and culinary properties. The young leaves have a distinct cucumber flavour and can be added to salads. Borage flowers are excellent for cut-flower arrangements or adding to drinks, salads, and desserts as a garnish. The blossoms are also a great favourite of honeybees. Borage grows well in most southern regions of Ontario.

VINTAGE ONTARIO BEVERAGES

Spruce Beer

Spruce beer has been known to Canadian settlers since the 1500s, when Jacques Cartier and his explorers were introduced to the beer, most likely by Indigenous Peoples. The fortress of Louisbourg on Cape Breton Island, Nova Scotia produced four-thousand barrels of spruce beer for its garrison of two-thousand troops in the 1750s. Hannah Jarvis (Queenston, Upper Canada) wrote about spruce beer in her housewifery book circa 1811. The beer was popular, in part, because spruce needles (a good source of Vitamin C) were known to help defend against scurvy. Spruce beer is currently enjoying a revival.

Spruce Beer

Take four ounces of hops, boil half an hour in one-gallon water, strain it, then add sixteen gallons warm water, two gallons molasses, eight ounces essence spruce* dissolved in one-quart water, put it in a clean cask, shake it well together, add half pint emptins**, let it stand one week, if very warm weather less time will do; when drawn off add one spoonful of molasses to each bottle.

* essence spruce – spruce boiled down in water until the water tastes of spruce
** a liquid leavening or starter, usually made at home from potatoes or hops and kept from one baking to the next (see the bread section for recipes for homemade starter)

Spruce Beer from *The Cook Not Mad*, 1831

Moose Milk

Though the origins of Moose Milk are rather obscure, legend has it that the drink was first served during an Officers' Mess at Canadian Forces Base Borden, Ontario, during the Second World War. The Commanding Officer asked that a drink that might appeal to females be served. The result was Moose Milk, which appealed as much to the men as it did to the women. Whether the story is true or not, the drink remains an unofficial, traditional, and immensely popular drink at celebratory events of the Canadian Armed Forces.

The drink also appears at levees and New Year's Day celebrations throughout Canada. The Royal Canadian Navy, Royal Canadian Air Force, and Canadian Army all claim to have invented the drink. Various recipes include Canadian whisky, rum, vodka, Kahlua, raw eggs, ice cream, eggnog, maple syrup, and cream. All claim to be the correct version.

Moose Milk

1 litre good quality vanilla ice cream, softened slightly
2 cups cold coffee
1 cup each of Canadian whisky, dark rum, and Kahlua or Tia Maria
A pinch of ground nutmeg to serve

Whisk the ingredients together to a froth and dust with a touch of nutmeg.

CONVERSION CHART FOR OLD RECIPES

MEASUREMENTS	
Butter the size of a walnut	2 tbsp
Butter the size of a hen's egg	¼ cup
Dash or a pinch of salt	1/8 teaspoon
Salt spoon	¼ teaspoon
Wine glass	¼ cup
Gill	½ cup
Teacup	¾ cup
Pint	2 cups
Quart	2 pints or 4 cups
Gallon	4 quarts or 16 cups
Peck	2 gallons or 8 quarts or 32 cups
OVEN TEMPERATURES	
Very slow	250°F or 140°C
Slow	300-325°F or 150-160°C
Moderately slow or Warm	325-350°F or 160-175°C
Moderate	350-375°F or 175-190°C
Moderately hot	375–400°F or 190–200°C
Hot	400–450°F or 200–230°C
Very hot	450–500°F or 230–260°C
INGREDIENTS	
Eggs – eggs were smaller in the 1800s	Use 1 extra large egg in recipes calling for 2 eggs. 2 large eggs in a recipe calling for 3 eggs, etc.
Potash, pearlash	1 tsp of potash/pearlash = ½ tsp baking soda
Isinglass	A kind of gelatine derived from fish
Pumpion	Early term for pumpkin
Saleratus	1 tsp saleratus = 1¼ tsp baking soda
Shortening	Any fat that is solid at room temperature: butter, margarine, lard or all-vegetable shortening
Vegetable Marrow	Similar to a very large, mature zucchini
White soup stock	Stock made from poultry and veal bones. Can substitute chicken or vegetarian stock
Yeast cake	2 ¼ tsp dry yeast or 1 pkg dry yeast
COOKING APPARATUS	
Bake Kettle	A large cast iron pot with a lid
Spider	Cast iron frying pan with three legs

ENDNOTES

1. Brandt, S., "The Evolution of Cooking Drove Evolution of the Human Species," *The Harvard Gazette*, 01 June 2009.

2. Museum of Ontario Archaeology, London, ON. http://diggingontario.uwo.ca/Palaeo.html

3. Humphreys, H., *The Ghost Orchard*: The Hidden History of the Apple in North America, Toronto: HarperCollins, 2017, p 13.

4. Langton, H.H., Ed., *A Gentlewoman in Upper Canada*: The Journals of Anne Langton, Toronto: Clarke, Irwin & Company Limited, 1950, p 36.

5. Moodie, S., *Roughing it In the Bush*; Or, Forest Life in Canada, Toronto: Maclear & Co., 1871, p 45.

6. *Ibid.*, Chapter 6.

7. Agriculture and Agri-Food Canada, "From a single seed - Tracing the Marquis wheat success story in Canada to its roots in Ukraine," https://goo.gl/7Qg3dZ

8. Russell, Loris, S., "The First Canadian Cooking Stove," *Canada An Historical Magazine*, 3,2, December 1975, p 34-35.

9. Traill, C. P., *The Backwoods of Canada: Being Letters from the Wife of an Emigrant Officer, Illustrative of the Domestic Economy of British America*, London: C.Knight, 1836, p 320.

10. Smith, M., *A Geographical View of the Province of Upper Canada and Promiscuous Remarks on the Government*, Trenton: Moore and Lake, 1813.

11. Lafitau Father J.F., *Customs of the American Indians*, Vol II., p 60.

12. Lewis, M. and Clark, W., *Journals of the Lewis & Clark Expedition*, Nebraska: University of Nebraska, https://lewisandclarkjournals.unl.edu/.

13. Macnab, S., *The Diary of Sophia Macnab*, Hamilton: Watermark Communications, 1968, p 28.

14. Port Arthur and Fort William amalgamated to become Thunder Bay in 1970.

15. Broadfoot, B., *Ten Lost Years 1929-1939: Memories of Canadians Who Survived the Depression*, Toronto: McClelland & Stewart Ltd, 1997, p 240.

16. Van Steen, M., *Pauline Johnson: Her Life and Work*, Toronto: Musson Book Company, 1965, p 29.

17. Gray, C., *Flint & Feather, The Life and Times of E. Pauline Johnson*, Tekahiomwake, Toronto: HarperCollins, 2002 p 360.

18. *Ibid.*, p 360.

19. Van Steen, M., *Pauline Johnson*, p 26.

20. E. Pauline Johnson (Tekahionwake), *Flint and Feather*, Toronto: The Musson Book Company Ltd. 1917, p. 95. Originally published in *E. Pauline Johnson (Tekahionwake)*, Canadian Born, Toronto: Morang, 1903.

21. Glazebrook, G.P. DeT., *Life In Ontario: A Social History*, Toronto: University of Toronto Press, 1968, p 5.

22. Partikian, M.P. and Viaud, J.P, *100 Years of Canadian Railway Recipes*, Saint-Constant, QC: Exporail. 2014.

23. McIntyre, J., *Musings on the Banks of Canadian Thames*, Ingersoll: H. Rowland, 1884 p 111-12.

24. Troyer, G., Ed., *Every Comfort in the Wilderness. A personal journal, with excerpts from the housewifery book, diaries and letters of Hannah Jarvis*, Upper Canada 1792-1845, Toronto: Green Dragon Press, 1994.

25. Driver, E., *Culinary Landmarks: A Bibliography of Canadian Cookbooks*, 1825-1949, Toronto: University of Toronto Press, 2008, p 322.

26. McClung, Nellie, *The Stream Runs Fast: My Own Story*, Toronto: Thomas Allen Limited, 1945, p 246.

27. Jameson, Anna, B., *Sketches in Canada and Rambles Among the Red Men*, London: Longman, Brown, Green, and Longmans, 1852, p 240.

28. Ibid., p. 244

29. Jameson, Anna, B., *Winter Studies and Summer Rambles in Canada, Vol. 1*, New York: Wiley and Putnam, 1839, p 191.

30. Arliss, H., *Melodist, and Mirthful Olio: An Elegant Collection of the Most Popular Songs, Recitations, Glees, Du ets, &c., Vol.* 1, London, England: Printed and Published by H. Arliss, 35, Gutter Lane, Cheapside, 1828.

31. Glazebrook, G.P. de T., *Life in Ontario A Social History*, Toronto: University of Toronto Press, 1968, p 10.

32. *Ibid*, p 11.

33. Graves, D. E., Ed., *Merry Hearts Make Light Days: The War of 1812 Journal of Lieutenant John Le Couteur, 104th Foot*, Montreal: Robin Brass Studio, 2012, p 166.

34. Elder, Louise, PhD, in "The History of Canadian Canners Limited 1903-1986," for the Scientific Research Department, Burlington, ON: 1986.

35. Traill, C.P, *The Female Emigrant's Guide and hints for Canadian Housekeeping*, 1854, p 106.

36. Stoddart, A. M, *The Life of Isabella Bird: Mrs Bishop*, London: J. Murray, 1906, p 12.

37. Bird, Isabella, L., *The Englishwoman in America*, London: John Murray, 1856, p 207.

38. "Agricultural Biodiversity: Banks for Bean Counters," *The Economist*, 12 September 2015, p 54.

39. Parr, J., *Domestic Goods: The Material, the Moral, and the Economic in the Postwar Years*, Toronto: University of Toronto Press, 1999, Appendix 1.

40. Father Joseph Francois Lafitau, *Customs of the American Indians, Vol II.*

ACKNOWLEDGEMENTS

Serious gratitude to all those who allowed me to access their family recipes and stories, old family photographs, rare old cookbooks, and culinary history ephemera, including (in alphabetical order): Deborah Cardiff; Melissa Collver; Paul Fortier; Megan Gao of the Moose Factory Hospital; Glenna Green; Lorraine Hinsberger; Angela Jouris Saxe; Joanne Karaiskakis; Margi McKay, Onagottay for your insights into the foodways of the First Peoples; Céline Pépin; Patty Quackenbush; Wendy Reynolds, Beverly Soloway; Jamie Toeppner; Joan Willison; and Peter Woolstencroft.

Thank you to all the staff and volunteers at various libraries, museums, and archives around Ontario who helped me with this project, including: staff at the Kingston Frontenac Public Library for procuring hundreds of books for me; Kim Bell at the W.D. Jordan Special Collections Library, Queen's University, Kingston, ON; Ryan Kirkby and Heather Callaghan at the University of Guelph Library - Archival and Special Collections, Guelph, ON; Jennifer Lyons, Head Curator, and Jessica Chase, Assistant Curator, Museums of Prince Edward County, Picton, ON; Melissa Collver, Director, Heritage & Culture, Norfolk County; Owen Cooke, Archives Volunteer at Rideau Archives, North Gower, ON; Alexandra McEwen, Alexandra Clemence, and staff of Library and Archives Canada, Ottawa, ON; Staff at Trent University Archives; Julian Whittam at Upper Canada Village, Morrisburg, ON; Janet Kronick and Victoria Bick at Dundurn Castle, Hamilton, ON; and Alex McLean, Fort Henry, Kingston, ON.

My sincere gratitude to everyone at MacIntyre Purcell Publishing Inc., it has been a privilege to work with you. Thank you to Chris Benjamin, for copyediting and Denis Cunningham for design and layout.

To Susan Scott, Joanne Karaiskakis, Joy McNevin, Tammy Lloyd, Kate Kristiansen, Heather Pearson, Katharine Smithrim, Elizabeth Greene, Julie Allain-Jean, Céline Pépin, Jan Murphy, Helen Humphreys, Jackie King, Karen Rudie, and all the members of my book group – thank you all for the gift of your presence in my life while I was working on this book.

I would also like to acknowledge the multitude of talented writers who have written on the topic of Canadian culinary history and offer my gratitude to Christina Bates, who wrote the first *Out of Old Ontario Kitchens* in 1978. This is not an updated version of her book, rather it is part of a provincial series by MacIntyre Purcell Publishing Inc.

And last but not least – endless love and gratitude to my family.

IMAGE AND ILLUSTRATION CREDITS

Page 9. Cooking Class, Ladies College, Ottawa, August 1906, by William James Topley. Library and Archives Canada/Topley Studio Fonds/a042227.

Page 10. *Canadian grown apples: delight in every bite* /Series: Bulletin no. 35, Fruit Branch, Department of Agriculture, Canada. Ottawa, 1926. Courtesy, University of Guelph, Special Collections.

Page 13. Mill on the Gananocoui [ca. 1792], by Elizabeth Simcoe. Reference Code: F47-11-1-0-63. Archives of Ontario, I0006915.

Page 14. Map of Canada West 1855, from Colton, J. H., and Colton, G. W., *Colton's Atlas of the World Illustrating Physical and Political Geography*, Vol 1, New York, 1855 (First Edition).

Page 16. White Swan Yeast Cakes advertisement from the *Canadian Farm Cook Book*, 1911

Page 17. End view of John's house [on Sturgeon Lake, Upper] Canada,1837, by Anne Langton. Reference Code: F 1077-8-1-4-19, Archives of Ontario, I0008042.

Page 20. The Moodie Homes, from Moodie, S., *Roughing it in the Bush: or, Life in Canada*, London, England, Richard Bentley, 1852.

Page 21. Bake Kettle, from The Chown & Cunningham Co., of Kingston Ltd. Catalogue and Price List, 1890-91.

Page 24. Imperial Oxford Ranges advertisement from *Two Hundred and Fifty Recipes*, by Grace Church Brantford, Ontario, 1900.

Page 26. Values of Farm Property in Ontario, 1923. Archives of Ontario Library Collection, Call No: Govt Doc A Misc Box 2 No 7, Crown copyright. Printed with the permission of the Archives of Ontario.

Page 28. Annie Kadlutikafaaluk boiling water and baking bannock on "kudlie" (seal-oil lamp), from Library and Archives Canada/ Richard Harrington fonds/a112075. © Library and Archives Canada. Reproduced with the permission of Library and Archives Canada.

Page 29. Barbara Mary Sutcliffe photograph, family collection.

Page 30. *Cow Brand Cook Book and Facts Worth Knowing*, Church and Dwight Company, 1900.

Page 32. Bertha Louise White photograph and handwritten Golden Corn Cake recipe card, courtesy of Margi McKay.

Page 34, The Parker House Hotel Daily Menu, January 4, 1858, New York Public Library's Digital Library Collection.

Page 34/35. Parker House Rolls image and recipe, E.W. Gillett Company, *Royal Yeast Bake Book*, 1920.

Page 37. Proud homeowners, Alex Kouhi and Lempi Koski Kouhi, photograph and Grandma Lempi's Pulla recipe courtesy of Beverly Soloway

Page 41. Canuck Rolled Oats advertisement from The Canadian Grocer, October to December 1913.

Page 42. Barm Brack recipe, Author unknown, Manuscript Cook Book, Special Collections, Queen's University Library, circa 1840.

Page 43. Nasmith's Bread Delivery Wagon, Earlscourt, Toronto, 1907, City of Toronto Archives, Fonds 1244 Item 31.

Page 44. Beckert's Garden, Field and Flower Seeds Catalog , Front Cover, W.G. Beckert, Allegheny, Pa. 1903.

Page 49. Map of British India, from Pope, G. U., *Text-book of Indian History: Geographical Notes, Genealogical Tables, Examination Questions*, London: W. H. Allen & Co. Pp. vii, 574, 16 maps, 1880.

Page 51. Clan Fraser Dinner Cover and Menu: "Clan Fraser, Souvenir of the first annual gathering, Toronto, May 5th, 1894. By Alexander Fraser. Toronto: Mail Job Printing Company, 1895."

Page 53. *Elizabeth Posthuma (Gwillim) Simcoe (1762-1850)*, by Mary Anne Burges, Library and Archives Canada, Ref. No. C-081931.

Page 54 - Bark Canoe sketch from, Powers, M. (Yeh Sen Noh Wehs), *Stories the Iroquois Tell Their Children*, New York: American Book Company, 1917.

Page 56. Mascalonge, from Henshall, J. A., *Bass, Pike, Perch, and Others*, New York: The Macmillan company, 1903.

Page 58. Food Lineups at the Yonge Street Mission during the Great Depression, Unknown photographer - Public Domain. Wikimedia Commons.

Page 59. Robert Evans and Co., Hamilton, ONT, Seed Catalogue 1897, Smithsonian Institution, Libraries Catalog No. 00038.

Page 60. E. Pauline Johnson, 1895, by Charles Scriber Cochran, Library and Archives Canada/Library of Parliament fonds/c085125k.

Page 62. Dreer's Garden Calendar 1884, by Henry A. Dreer (Firm); Henry G. Gilbert Nursery and Seed Trade Catalog Collection, 1884.

Page 65. Dandelion family, Barton, B. H. and Castle, T., *The British Flora Medica, or, History of the medicinal plants of Great Britain*, London: E Cox, 1838.

Page 68. Salsify, Peter Henderson & Co, Manual of Everything for the Garden, New York, Peter Henderson & Co., Henry G. Gilbert Nursery and Seed Trade Catalog Collection 1884.

Page 70. Fèves au lard (baked beans) recipe and translation, courtesy of Celine Pepin.

Page 71. Heinz Beans Streetcar Advertisement, Leamington, ON., 1910, used with permission from the Senator John Heinz History Center, Pittsburgh, PA, USA.

Page 72. Ruth Marian White 1924 photograph and Carrot Soufflé recipe courtesy of Margi McKay.

Page 73. Varieties of Carrots: D.M. Ferry & Co; Seed Annual 1916, Detroit, Michigan: Henry G. Gilbert Nursery and Seed Trade Catalog Collection, 1916.

Page 74. "Cheese" from: *Mrs. Beeton's Book of Household Management*, 1906.

Page 75. Mammoth Cheese made at Ingersoll, C.W. 1866. Library and Archives Canada/James A. Crawford fonds/c008564.

Page 76. Mammoth Cheese leaving Perth, April 1893, Library and Archives Canada/Donald C. Beckett collection/a160538.

Page 77. Poster advertising the Mammoth Cheese, 1893, Library and Archives Canada/Donald C. Beckett collection/ a160537.

Page 79. "The Rabbit" from: Tarbox, I.N., *Aunt Ellen's Visit to Little Mary*, New York: Leavitt & Allen Publishers, 1855.

Page 81. Hannah Owen Jarvis (née Peters) with her daughters Maria Lavinia and Augusta Honoria Jarvis, by James Earl, between circa 1791 and circa 1792, Royal Ontario Museum, Accession number 981.79.2, accessed via Wikimedia Commons.

Page 82. Two Hens and a Rooster, circa 1828, from thegraphicsfairy.com.

Page 83. Canada's Egg Opportunity WWI poster, 1918, Canada Food Board, C233-2-2-0-66, Archives of Ontario.

Page 84. There is a World Famine of Beef, Bacon and Wheat poster, Library and Archives Canada/National Archives of Canada fonds/e010697130.

Page 85. Nellie McClung, 1914, by Cyril Jessop, Library and Archives Canada/Canadian Intellectual Property Office fonds/a030212.

Page 87. Cottolene Shortening Advertisement, circa 1868, courtesy Museums of Prince Edward County.

Page 88. Anna Brownell Jameson, date and artist unknown. Courtesy of Toronto Public Library.

Page 88. Canoe on Lake Huron by Anna Brownell Jameson, 1837. Courtesy of Toronto Public Library.
Page 89. Brown Trout (*Salmo trutta fario*) by Duane Raver, U.S. Fish and Wildlife Service, date unknown. Accessed by Wikimedia Commons.

Page 92. Nettie Jane (Wallace) Leonard photograph and "How to Cook Deer" manuscript cookbook page, courtesy of Wendy Reynolds.

Page 94. Ardwold Circa 1910, City of Toronto Archives, Fonds 1244, Item 316.

Page 103. Lady Susan Agnes Macdonald, wife of Sir John A. Macdonald, Ottawa, May 1868, by William James Topley, Library and Archives Canada/Topley Studio Fonds/a026285.

Page 105. Ken Mechefske and Margaret Lang circa 1945 photograph from a family collection.

Page 109. Are you breaking the Law? Patriotic Canadians Will Not Hoard Food: Canada Food Board sensitive campaign, WWI, Library and Archives Canada/National Archives of Canada fonds/e010697116.

Page 110. George Walker Collver and Allie Winnifred (Nelles) Collver photograph and "Supper Dish," manuscript cookbook page courtesy of Melissa Collver.

Page 113. Female Land Locked Salmon, by Sherman Foote Denton, from the Second Annual Report of the Commissioners of Fisheries, Game and Forests of the State of New York, 1896, New York City (NY): Wynkoop Hallenbeck Crawford Co., Printers, 1897.

Page 115. Ontario Canning Labels, Prince Edward County, courtesy Museums of Prince Edward County.

Page 116. Jell-O Canada's Most Favourite Dessert, Jell-O Recipe Pamphlet from Bridgeburg, ON, circa 1910-1914, private collection.

Page 117. Wild Rice Harvest, from Traill, C. P., *The Female Emigrant's Guide and hints for Canadian Housekeeping*, 1854.

Page 118. Five of seventeen Hummel family siblings, circa 1901, photograph courtesy of Lorraine Hinsberger.

Page 119. Trout Creek, Ontario, circa 1900, photograph (from the collection of Vic Kelly) used with the permission of Jamie Toeppner. http://www.toeppner.ca/vic_kelly/index.html.

Page 121. *Manuscript cookbook of Rachel (Hummel) Lang*, courtesy of Andy Lang.

Page 123. Pudding Illustrations, from, *Mrs. Beeton's Every Day Cookery and Housekeeping Book*, 1893.

Page 126. King George I, 1713, by Sir Godfrey Kneller, National Portrait Gallery London, UK, accessed by Wikimedia Commons.

Page 127. The Empire Christmas Pudding: A Christmas Pudding Recipe, Library and Archives Canada/National Archives of Canada fonds/e010697116.

Page 130. The Ladies of Kingston are delighted with sunlight baking powder advertisement, from St. Andrew's Presbyterian Church Young Women's Guild, *Tried and True Recipes, Kingston*, ON: 1910.

Page 133. Elderberry botanical illustration, from Wagner, D., *Pharmaceutisch medizinische Botanik*, Vienna, Austria: 1828-1830.

Page 135. Magdalena Buzzard and Luella (Buzzard) Erb family photographs and recipe courtesy of Deborah Cardiff.

Page 138. *Economy Recipes for Canada's "Housoldiers"* from the Canada Starch Company, 1943.

Page 140. "McIntosh Apple," by Deborah Griscom Passmore, Plate XLVII from the Yearbook of the United States Department of Agriculture, 1901.

Page 142. Adelaide Hunter Hoodless, 43 cent postage stamp, Canada Post © 1993. Reproduced with permission.

Page 145. Canada War Cake recipe courtesy of Glenna Green.

Page 147. Joan Langford Lavery photograph and Nana Langford's Gum Drop Cake recipe courtesy of Joanne Karaiskakis.

Page 148. Cowan's Cake Icings advertisement from the Canadian Farm Cook Book, 1911.
Page 151. Butternut Tree (*Juglans cinerea*) Plate XXXII from: Bigelow, J. (1786-1879) *American Medical Botany, Vol. 1.*, Boston, Massachusetts: Cummings and Hilliard, 1817.

Page 152. Early twentieth-century dinner cards from the scrapbooks of Belle Botsford Scott. Source: Library and Archives Canada/Arthur Stanley Bourinot fonds/ LMS-0014/Accession 1971-01, box 54, book 2, p. 333.

Page 156. Joan (Langford) Lavery's handwritten Matrimonial Cake recipe courtesy of Joanne Karaiskakis.

Page 157. Hotpoint Stove advertisement, *Lord Salisbury I.O.D.E Cook Book*, Toronto, 1923.

Page 160. Bertha White's Empire Biscuits handwritten recipe card, courtesy of Margi McKay.

Page 161. Cutting Ice on the River, Toronto, Ontario, 1890s, Archives of Ontario, C 7-3 545.

Page 163. Label for Canadian Tomato Chutnee endorsed by Sir John A. Macdonald, Library and Archives Canada/Morris Norman collection/e008072633.

Page 172. Eno's Fruit Salt: The Natural Health Drink advertisement from: *Lord Salisbury I.O.D.E Cook Book*, Toronto, 1923.

Page 175. Choice Small Fruit, from Henry G. Gilbert Nursery and Seed Catalog, Springfield, OH: Geo. H. Mullen Co., 1904.

BIBLIOGRAPHY

(The) Alexandra Club of Pembroke, *The Alexandra Club Cook Book*, Pembroke, ON: The Alexandra Club, (Printers: Foster and North Limited, Kingston, ON), 1952.

Anon., (Compiled by the Women's Department, Canadian Farm) *Canadian Farm Cook Book*, Toronto: Canadian Farm, 1911.

Anon., (Compiled by The Ladies of Toronto and Chief Cities and Towns in Canada), *The Home Cook Book*, Toronto: Hunter, Rose and Company, 1877.

Anonymous, *The Canadian Housewife's Manual of Cookery: Carefully Compiled from the Best English, French & American Works, Especially Adapted to this Country*, Hamilton, Canada West: Printed by William Gillespy, Henry L Richards, "Spectator" Office, 1861.

Anon., *The Cook Not Mad; Or Rational Cookery*, Kingston, Upper Canada: James Macfarlane, 1831. [Bicentennial Edition reprinted by The Cherry Tree Press, Toronto, 1984.

Arliss, H., Melodist, and Mirthful Olio: An Elegant Collection of the Most Popular Songs, Recitations, Glees, Duets, &c., Vol. 1, London, England: Printed @ Publ by H. Arliss, 35, Gutter Lane, Cheapside, 1828.

Author unknown, *Manuscript Cook Book*, Special Collections, Queen's University Library, circa 1840.

Bank Street Church Ladies' Association, *The Canadian Economist: a book of tried and tested receipts: the profits to be devoted to the church.* Ottawa: A. Mortimer, 1881.

Bates, C., *Out of Old Ontario Kitchens: A collection of traditional recipes of Ontario and the stories of the people who cooked them*, Toronto: Pagurian Press, 1978.

Beeton, I., *Mrs. Beeton's Book of Household Management*, London, England: S.O Beeton Publishing, 1861.

Beeton, I., *Mrs. Beeton's Cookery Book*, London, England, Ward, Lock and Co., 1912

Bird, I.L., *The Englishwoman in America*, London: John Murray, 1856.

Blue Ribbon Manufacturing Company, *Blue Ribbon and Pure Gold Cook Book*, 18th Edition, Winnipeg, MB: Blue Ribbon Mfg Co., 1905.

Board of Education, Toronto, *Handbook of Practical Cookery for the Use of Household Science Classes: in the Public Schools of Toronto*, Toronto: Board of Education, 1937.

Broadfoot, B., *Ten Lost Years 1929-1939: Memories of Canadians Who Survived the Depression*, Toronto: McClelland & Stewart Ltd, 1997.

Coburg Congregational Church Ladies' Aid, *The Cobourg Congregational cook book*: a selection of tested recipes,

Cobourg, ON: Ladies' Aid of the Cobourg Congregational Church, 1909.

Denison, G. E., The Canadian Family Cook Book: a volume of tried, tested and proven recipes, Toronto: George McLeod, 1914.

Dreer, H. A., *Dreer's Garden Calendar 1884*, Philadelphia, Pa.: Henry A. Dreer, 1884.

Driver, E., *Culinary Landmarks: A Bibliography of Canadian Cookbooks*, 1825-1949, Toronto: University of Toronto Press, Scholarly Publishing Division, 2008.

Dufferin, Lady, *My Canadian Journal 1872-1878*, Edited and annotated by Gladys C. Walker, Don Mills, ON: Longmans Canada Limited, 1969.

Duncan, D, *Canadians at Table: A Culinary History of Canada*, Toronto: Dundurn Press, 2006
.

E.W. Gillett Company, *Royal Yeast Bake Book*, Toronto: E.W. Gillett Company, 1920.

Fairfield, D. E., *Dora's Cook Book*, Toronto: Hunter, Rose & Co., 1888.

Family Herald and Weekly Star, *The Family Herald Cook Book*, Montreal: The Family Herald and Weekly Star, 1924.

Farmer, F. M., *The Boston Cooking-School Cook Book*, Boston: Little, Brown, & Company, 1911.

Glasse, H., *The Art of Cookery Made Plain and Easy*, London: 1747. https://archive.org/details/TheArtOfCookery

Glazebrook, G.P. DeT., *Life In Ontario: A Social History*, Toronto: University of Toronto Press, 1968

Grace Church Sewing Circle, *Two Hundred and Fifty Recipes*, Brantford, ON: Donovan & Henwood, 1900

Graves, D. E., Editor, *Merry Hearts Make Light Days: The War of 1812 Journal of Lieutenant John Le Couteur, 104th Foot*, Second Edition, Montreal: Robin Brass Studio Inc., 2012.

Gray, C., Flint & Feather: *The Life and Times of E. Pauline Johnson*, Tekahionwake, Toronto: HarperCollins Publishers Ltd., 2002.

Hoodless, Mrs. J., (Adelaide), *Public School Domestic Science*, Toronto: The Copp, Clark Company, Limited, 1898.

Humphreys, H., *The Ghost Orchard: The Hidden History of the Apple in North America*, Toronto: HarperCollins, 2017.

Jameson, A.B., *Winter Studies and Summer Rambles in Canada*, London, England: Saunders and Otley, 1838, Facsimile Edition, Toronto, Coles Publishing Company, 1972.

Johnson, E. P., (Tekahionwake, *Flint and Feather*, Toronto, The Musson Book Company Ltd. 1917.

Lafitau, Fr. J. F., *Customs of the American Indians, Vol II.*, edited by Fenton, W.N. and Moore, E.L., Toronto: The Champlain Society, 1974.

Langton, H. H., Editor, *A Gentlewoman in Upper Canada: The Journals, Letters and Art of Anne Langton*, Toronto: Clarke, Irwin & Company Limited, 1950.

Lewis, M. and Clark, W., *Journals of the Lewis & Clark Expedition*, Nebraska: University of Nebraska, https://lewisandclarkjournals.unl.edu/.

Macdonald, Lady Susan A., *The Manuscript Receipt Book and Household Treasury*, Ottawa: J. Durie & Son, circa 1860

Macnab, S., *The Diary of Sophia Macnab*, Hamilton: Watermark Communications, 1968

McClung, N. L., *Clearing in the West*, Toronto: Thomas Allen, 1935

McClung, N., L., *The Stream Runs Fast*, Toronto: Thomas Allen, 1945

McDougall, W., and Buckland G., *Canadian Agriculturist*, Toronto: Board of Agriculture of Upper Canada, Rowsell & Thompson, 1848-1863.

McIntyre, J., *Musings on the Banks of Canadian Thames*, Ingersoll: H. Rowland, 1884

Mechefske, L., *Sir John's Table: The Culinary Life and Times of Canada's First Prime Minister*, Fredericton, NB: Goose Lane Editions, 2015.

Metropolitan Life Insurance Company, *The Metropolitan Life cook book*, Ottawa: Metropolitan Life Insurance Co., 1918.

Mosby, I., *Food Will Win the War*, Vancouver: UBC Press, 2014.

Moodie, S., *Roughing it in the Bush: or, Forest Life in Canada*, London, England, Richard Bentley, 1852.

Navy League Chapter I.O.D.E., *Victory Cook Book*, Victoria: Victoria Printing and Publishing, 1941

Nourse, E., *Modern Practical Cookery, Pastry, Confectionery, Pickling and Preserving: With a Great Variety of Useful and Economic Receipts*, Montreal: Armour & Ramsay, 1845.

Ogilvie Flour Mills Company, *Ogilvie's Book for a Cook*, Montreal, Ogilvie Flour Mills Company Ltd., 1931.

Opti-Mrs. Club of Kingston, *Opti-Mrs. Cook Book*, Kingston: Opti-Mrs. Club of Kingston, ON, 1950.

Parr, J., Domestic Goods: *The Material, the Moral, and the Economic in the Postwar Years*, Toronto: University of Toronto Press, 1999

Partikian, M.P. & Viaud, J.P., *100 Years of Canadian Railway Recipes*, Saint-Constant, QC: Exporail. 2014

Pattison, N. L., *Canadian Cook Book*, Toronto: Ryerson Press, 1924

Powell, E.J. Mrs., *The Toronto Cook Book*, Toronto: printed by the Mortimer Company, 1915.

Purity Flour Mills Limited, *Purity Cook Book* (1932, Second Revision, January 1945), Toronto: Purity Flour Mills Limited, 1945.

Rees, M. H. (Dietician, Compiled by), *Tasty Meals for Every Day*, Toronto: Canada Packers Limited, 1933.

Scott, A. L., *The New Purity Cook Book: The Complete Guide to Canadian Cooking*, Toronto: Maple Leaf Mills Ltd., 1965

Simcoe, E. P., (Ed. Innis, Mary Quayle) *Mrs. Simcoe's Diary*, Toronto: Dundurn Press, 2007.

Simcoe, E.P., and Robertson, J. R., *The diary of Mrs. John Graves Simcoe, wife of the first lieutenant-governor of the province of Upper Canada*, 1792-6, Toronto: W. Briggs, 1911.

Smith, M., *A Geographical View of the Province of Upper Canada and Promiscuous Remarks on the Government*, Trenton: Moore and Lake, 1813.

Standard Brands Ltd, *The Magic Cook Book*, Toronto: Standard Brands Limited (Gillett Products), 1930.

St. Andrew's Presbyterian Church Young Women's Guild, *Tried and True Recipes*, Kingston, ON: 1910.

St. Luke's Women's Auxiliary, *Culinary Landmarks: Or Half-Hours with Sault Ste. Marie Housewives*, 3rd Edition, Sault Ste. Marie: 1909.

Stoddart, A. M., *The Life of Isabella Bird (Mrs Bishop)*, London: J. Murray, 1906

Taylor, M. and McNaught, F., Eds., *The New Galt Cook Book*, Toronto: McLeod and Allen, 1898

Traill, C. P., *Female Emigrant's Guide and Hints on Canadian Housekeeping*, Toronto: MacLear and Company, 1854.

Traill, C. P., *The Backwoods of Canada: Being letters from the wife of an emigrant officer: Illustrative of the domestic economy of British America*, London, England, C. Knight, 1836.

Troyer, G., Ed., *Every Comfort in the Wilderness. A personal journal, with excerpts from the housewifery book, diaries and letters of Hannah Jarvis, Upper Canada 1792-1845*, Toronto: Green Dragon Press, 1994.

Van Steen, *M., Pauline Johnson: Her Life and Work*, Toronto: Musson Book Company, 1965.

Watkins Cook Book. J.R. Watkins Co., Winona, Minnesota, 1925.

Wellington Community Historical Museum, *Pickle Recipes from the Last 125 Years*, printed by the Wellington Community Historical Museum, Prince Edward County, Ontario, date unknown.

Wesley United Church Good Cheer Club, (Compiled by), *Cook to Win*, Calgary: Wesley United Church, 1943.

Wimodausis Club, *The Wimodausis Club Cook Book*, Toronto: Hunter, Rose & Co., 1922

Women's Auxiliary to Royal Victoria Hospital (Compilers), *Royal Victoria Cook Book*, Barrie: S. Wesley, 1900.

Women's Auxiliary of the Y.M.C.A., *Cook Book: recipes tested and tried*, Woodstock, ON: 1909

Zion United Church Women's Association, *Zion Cook Book*, Kingston, ON: The Gananoque Reporter: Printers to the People, circa 1929.

Journals and Occasional Papers

Board of Agriculture of Upper Canada, *The Canadian Agriculturalist*, Toronto: W. McDougall, G. Buckland, 1848-1863.

Brandt, S., "The Evolution of Cooking Drove Evolution of the Human Species," *The Harvard Gazette*, 01 June 2009

Department of Agriculture, Canada, Fruit Branch, *Canadian grown apples: delight in every bite* /Series: Bulletin no. 35, Ottawa, 1926.

Elder, Louise. *"The History of Canadian Canners Limited"*, 1903-1986. Hamilton, ON: Canadian Canners, 1986.

Russell, Loris, S., "The First Canadian Cooking Stove," *Canada An Historical Magazine*, Vol. 3,2, December 1975, p 34-35.

The Canadian Grocer, Toronto: Maclean-Hunter Publ. Co. 1887-1913.

INDEX OF RECIPES